The Hidden Life
of Dogs

Books by
Elizabeth Marshall Thomas

FICTION

Reindeer Moon
The Animal Wife

NONFICTION

The Harmless People
Warrior Herdsmen
The Hidden Life of Dogs

Elizabeth Marshall Thomas

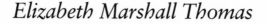

The Hidden Life of Dogs

A PETER DAVISON BOOK

HOUGHTON MIFFLIN COMPANY

BOSTON / NEW YORK

For information about permission to reproduce
selections from this book, write to Permissions,
Houghton Mifflin Company, 215 Park Avenue South,
New York, New York 10003.

Library of Congress Cataloging-in-Publication Data

Thomas, Elizabeth Marshall, date.
The hidden life of dogs / Elizabeth Marshall Thomas ;
[illustrations by Jared T. Williams].
p.   cm.
"A Peter Davison book."
Includes bibliographical references.
ISBN 0-395-66958-8
1. Dogs — Behavior.   2. Dogs — Psychology.   I. Title.
SF433.T47   1993   93-18289
599.74'422 — dc20   CIP

Printed in the United States of America

BP 19 18 17 16 15 14

Book design by Robert Overholtzer

Illustrations by Jared T. Williams

To Lorna Marshall,

MY MOTHER

THIS IS A BOOK about dog consciousness. To some people, the subject might seem anthropomorphic simply by definition, since in the past even scientists have been led to believe that only human beings have thoughts or emotions. Of course, nothing could be further from the truth. Surely, that such a notion remains in our philosophy is merely a holdover from the Christian creationism it resembles, and is unscientific at that, given the fact that human beings have consciousness which, in the absence of miracles, we acquired through our long mammalian past. Hence, while the question of animal consciousness is a perfectly valid field for scientific exploration, the general assumption that other creatures lack consciousness is astonishing.

After all, thoughts and emotions have evolutionary value. If they didn't, we wouldn't have them. Thought is an efficient, effective mechanism that we, and many other animals, would be hard put to do without. With intellect, which is to say the ability to learn and reason, an organism such as a person or a dog can cope with a wide variety of problems that would require an enormous amount of hard-wiring if the behavioral solution to each problem were pre-programmed. When we relegate animal thought to instinct, we overlook the fact that instinct is merely an elegant matrix for the formation of an intellect, a fail-safe device that guides each species to form thoughts. When shaped by education, our thoughts enable us to do what we do, and even to be what we are, not only as members of our species but as individuals.

As for consciousness, consider the four following observations: the first of a dog's custom, the second of a dog weighing two alternatives, the third of a dog playing a game, and the fourth of a dog who figured out and temporarily adopted a human mannerism. The dog's custom was started in a household in Boulder, Colorado, by five dogs who, unlike any other dogs this author has ever seen, ate lying down. They certainly had not been trained to do this — on the contrary, the owners found nothing remarkable about the custom and in fact seemed touchingly unaware that other dogs ate differently. Why did these dogs eat lying down? No one knew for sure. The alpha dog, a male Australian shepherd named Rider, had apparently started the custom, perhaps to reduce excitement and competition at mealtimes, when his owners, busy parents with five children and overloaded schedules, would plunk down five bowls of kibbles in the yard and get on with the next urgent matter. Thus the dogs had to police themselves. Quickly choosing a bowl, each dog would lie down and eat the food. Later, almost as if at a signal, all would get up and move around, licking out one another's dishes. Giving the impression that they considered their behavior perfectly ordinary, the dogs invariably left human observers perplexed.

Yet it is possible to guess at a reason for the custom: Rider is frailer than two of the others, both hefty females with barrel bodies and Percheron hips. One is significantly older than Rider, and both are excitable when mealtimes come. Hence, I believe, the potential for crowding and shouldering is high at mealtimes, especially on days when the task of feeding falls to the family's teenage son, who has more interesting things on his mind than household chores. As a result, the dogs know all about waiting. In their yard, the afternoon wears on, and the sun creeps toward the Rockies. Feeding time comes, but nothing happens. Soon the sky is dark, but still no one comes. At last the neighborhood is quiet. Lights go on in the houses. The neighboring families gather in their kitchens. But in one yard, hunger and anxiety are mounting.

Did the uncertain atmosphere contribute to the custom? Could the dogs have sought to defuse the potentially flammable situation that arises when at last the kibbles rattle into the bowls? The five dogs don't recline at ease, as if to enhance enjoyment; rather, they lie stiffly, bowls between their forelegs, elbows flat, chests touching the ground, bellies slightly arched, knees up, and hocks down. They look like dogs down on command at obedience school. In this position they eat quickly and quietly, occasionally glancing at one another from the corners of their eyes. The custom makes for a controlled, orderly mealtime instead of a free-for-all in which the small but intelligent Rider could be steamrollered by the taller and heavier females.

Eventually, Rider's daughter, young Pearl, was sent to New England to join two older dogs in a household where pets were fed morning and evening. For a while, Pearl retained her unusual custom as best she could, standing up to eat the morning meal but dutifully lying down to eat the evening meal as she would have done back in Boulder. Even so, she soon gave up, and the strange custom never took root. If Pearl had been the alpha dog, it might have. But in her new home she wasn't even the alpha dog's daughter. Instead, her status was low, and the two old dogs didn't emulate her. So, after a few weeks, she chose to emulate them, and from then on stood up to eat both meals just as they did.

The dog who was observed weighing alternatives and making a decision was also a young female. Every day this dog took a walk with her owner and two other dogs, and every day they stopped at a river, where the young female invariably had a swim. On the day in question, however, something off the trail had drawn the young female away from the group, so that when the others stopped at the river, she wasn't with them. They turned to go home, as was their custom, and had gone about eighty feet down the trail when the young female, hot and ready for her daily bath, burst out of the bushes halfway between them and the river. Too late — they were leaving, and she had missed her swim. Poised beside the trail, she first looked to the right after her group, then looked to the left at the river, then looked to the right a second time, then looked once more at the water, made an instant decision, rushed full speed up the trail to the river, plunged in, quickly swam a few strokes, then turned back to the bank, leaped out, and tore after her group, not stopping to shake until she had caught up to them. (Virtually all dogs wait to shake themselves until they rejoin their group, especially if the others of the group did not swim; the need to shake seems secondary to the need to be close after having had a notably different experience from the others.)

The dog who was observed playing a game was a young male, a shepherd-Lab cross who had recently been given to an inactive, somewhat elderly couple who also owned an inactive, elderly female dog. The youngster had no one to play with — certainly not the older dog, who was very strict with him and tolerated no amusement of any kind. So the poor young dog often seemed at a loss, like a young person with no friends and nothing to do. One snowy night I saw him all by himself on a hillside near the house where he was staying, running fast with his nose to the ground. Whatever little rodent he was chasing seemed to be leading him in a big circle, which returned the rodent to the starting point, where the dog nuzzled for quite a while in one place — evidently at a hole where the quarry had gone to earth. But then, to my surprise, the dog started running again. Again with his nose to the ground, he made a second big circle that retraced the first. And again he nuzzled in one place, as if his quarry had again gone to earth.

I found all this very strange. What little creature would come up out of a safe hole right under a dog's nose in order to lead the dog around in a circle? And wouldn't the dog grab it when it came out? While I was puzzling over this, the dog rushed around the circle a third time, then a fourth, then a fifth and sixth. Each time his demeanor was the same — alert, excited, tail high and waving, nose to earth, as eager the last time as he had been the first. And when I went near for a look, I found, of course, that there was no quarry, and no hole either. The entire event had been a fantasy. This imaginative dog had been pretending.

The dog who adopted a human mannerism is my husband's dog, who amazed us all one hot day this past summer after my husband had bought himself an ice cream cone. As my husband took the first taste, he noticed that his dog was watching. So he offered the cone, expecting the dog to gobble it. But to everyone's astonishment, the dog politely licked a little ice cream just as my husband had done. My husband then licked a little more, and again offered it to the dog, who also licked a little more. In this way, taking turns, they ate the ice cream down to the cone. Then my husband took a bite. The dog watched him. Assuming that the dog would bolt the rest of the cone, my husband passed it on for what he thought would be the last time. But drawing back his lips to expose his little incisors, the dog took the most delicate of nibbles. Twice more my husband and the dog took turns biting the cone, until only the tip remained.

Astounding? Not really. For eight years, my husband and this dog have built a relationship of trust and mutual obligation, neither making unreasonable demands on the other or patronizing the other, or trying to subordinate the other, but each doing exactly what he wants, usually in the other's company. Only in such a setting, only when both participants consider themselves equals, could this scene have taken place. Only a dog who thought for himself, a dog who wasn't brainwashed by excessive training, a dog who depended on his own observations and imagination for guidance, would ever figure out the very human method of taking alternate bites as a form of sharing. After all, when two dogs share food, they eat simultaneously while respecting each other's feeding space, which is a little imaginary circle around the other's mouth. But the idea of taking alternate bites is totally human. Even so, the dog fathomed it, *and without ever having seen it done.* Who ate the tip of the cone? My husband ate it. The dog let him have the last turn.

Do dogs have thoughts and feelings? Of course they do. If they didn't, there wouldn't be any dogs. That being said, however, a book on dogs must by definition be somewhat anthropomorphic, and reasonably so, since our aversion to the label is misplaced. Using the experience of one's species to evaluate the experience of another species has been a useful tool to many of the great wildlife biologists. The more experienced the investigator, the more useful the tool. Consider George Schaller's observation of a mother leopard and her son: "At times [the two leopards] had ardent reunions, rubbing their cheeks and bodies sinuously and licking each other's face, obviously excited and delighted with the meeting. Witnessing such tenderness, I realized that these leopards merely masked their warm temperament and emotional depth beneath a cold exterior."*

In contrast is the observation of a former neighbor of mine, now deceased — a psychiatrist, actually — who saw a bird fly into the glass of his

---

* George Schaller, *Golden Shadows, Flying Hooves* (New York: Knopf, 1973), p. 196.

picture window and fall to earth, stunned. In a moment, a second bird swooped down, picked up the first, and flew away with it. In a quite moving anthropomorphization, the psychiatrist assumed that the second bird was a male, the mate of the first, and had come to her rescue. However, since birds never carry their loved ones, and grab other birds only to kill them, the second bird was surely not a helper at all but a predator taking advantage of the first bird's plight. If the psychiatrist had been more familiar with the ways of the natural world, he probably wouldn't have made that particular assumption.

We are not the only species to apply our values and our experience when interpreting other creatures. Dogs do it too, sometimes with no more luck than the psychiatrist. When a dog with a bone menaces a human observer, the dog actually assumes that the person wants the slimy, dirt-laden object, and is applying dog values, or cynomorphizing. Nevertheless, most animals, including dogs, constantly evaluate other species by means of empathetic observation. A dog of mine once assessed my mood, which was dark, over a distance of about one hundred yards, and changed his demeanor from cheery to bleak in response. He was in a pen that I was approaching, and as I rounded the corner he caught sight of me. I was sad at heart but not show-ing it in a way that any of the people around me had noticed, but the dog saw at once that something was wrong. Over the great distance he stared at me a moment, as if to be sure that he was really seeing what he thought he was seeing, and then, evidently deciding that his first impression had been accurate, he drooped visibly. I was so impressed with his acu-ity that I cheered up again, and so did he!

I was equally impressed by a female housecat, Lilac, whom I happened to be carrying home one evening, when on the way I decided to look in a nearby field to see if by chance any deer were graz-ing. I must have tensed a little as I got near the field, and perhaps walked a bit more quietly, but whatever it was, Lilac felt the change, instantly rec-ognized it as a prelude to hunting, and leaned for-ward, ears up, eyes wide, claws sticking into my arm, ready to spring at whatever I might be stalking.

As a further note on anthropomorphism, the reader may notice references herein to a dog's smile. All dogs smile, which is to say their faces become pleasant and relaxed, with ears low, eyes half shut, lips soft and parted, and chin high. This is a dog smile. Yet a few dogs also emulate human smiles, and hence they themselves are anthropomorphizing. In the presence of human beings these dogs will draw back their lips grotesquely to bare their teeth, making the same face we make. At the same time, these dogs may also roll over to reveal their bellies submissively, showing that they understand exactly what our smiles mean.

And finally, anthropomorphism can help us interpret the act of showing the belly — the act that symbolizes what puppies do when submitting to adult dogs. By the act, dogs say to us, *Do as you will with us, since we are helpless puppies in your presence.* To understand the act, we can look at the human parallel: the way many religious people — Christians, for example — behave toward God. We call God the parent and ourselves his children. When we kneel to pray, we diminish our height, so that we look more like young children. Our prayerful position with raised eyes suggests that we are clasping God around the knees and looking up, as if he were facing us and looking straight down, not as if he were, say, off on the horizon. What's more, just as many of us pray at specified hours — upon getting up in the morning or going to bed at night, for instance — many dogs do their ritual submission at certain times of day. My husband's dog, for example, elects to show his belly to my husband right after they both get up in the morning. Why? No one knows for sure, but by now they both expect it.

Do dogs think we're God? Probably not. But just as we think of God's ways as mysterious, dogs find our ways capricious and mysterious, often with excellent reason. Every day the humane societies execute thousands of dogs who tried all their lives to do their very best by their owners. These dogs are killed not because they are bad but because they are inconvenient. So as we need God more than he needs us, dogs need us more than we need them, and they know it.

I have tried, in the pages that follow, to record the lives of a group of eleven dogs, five males and six females. Five of the dogs were born not merely in our house but right beside me on my bed, and ten of the dogs stayed with us throughout their natural lives, so I was able to witness much of what happened to them. I wanted to see what they would do when free to plan their own time and make their own decisions. However, I don't pretend that my experiment was scientific, or anything more than a casual (if lengthy) observation. Nor can I say that the dogs were free to act entirely naturally, since to a limited extent I controlled their roaming and their breeding. Because the population of unwanted dogs is the cause of immense pain and tragedy, the females were spayed, two without ever giving birth, three after having had one litter, and one after having had two litters.

Even so, twenty-two pups were born. Six died before reaching maturity. Of those who lived, we kept five and gave away eleven, all of whom were chosen by people we knew personally. I gave the pups away freely, since I strongly believe that even though dogs are slaves, it is nevertheless wrong to sell them. I wanted to keep track of each pup to ascertain its well-being for as long as possible, and was able to do so for nine of them. Of these, one vanished, and two died at about a year old, one hit by a car and one put down for a late-emerging birth defect. To the best of my knowledge, for at least three years five remained in their first homes and one went to a second home.

To the dogs who stayed with me I gave food, water, and shelter, but after my project began I made no effort to train them, even for housebreaking or coming when called. I didn't need to. The young dogs copied the old dogs, which in their case resulted in perfect housebreaking, and all the dogs naturally came when called most of the time, declining to do so only if our demands conflicted with something that was genuinely important to them. A dog who feels free to make such a distinction shows more of his thoughts and feelings in a single day than a rigidly trained, hyperdisciplined dog can show in a lifetime.

I count an hour watching a dog as an hour of observation, and an hour watching two dogs as two hours of observation. By this method of reckoning, I have logged in well over 100,000 hours since my project started, every one of which was fascinating. I will always live with dogs, and I will always watch them, so the process goes on.

The Hidden Life
of Dogs

I BEGAN observing dogs by accident. While friends spent six months in Europe, I took care of their husky, Misha. An agreeable two-year-old Siberian with long, thin legs and short, thick hair, Misha could jump most fences and travel freely. He jumped our fence the day I took him in. A law requiring that dogs be leashed was in effect in our home city of Cambridge, Massachusetts, and also in most of the surrounding communities. As Misha violated the law I would receive complaints about him, and with the help of these complaints, some from more than six miles distant, I soon was able to establish that he had developed a home range of approximately 130 square miles. This proved to be merely a preliminary home range, which later he expanded considerably, but interestingly enough, even young Misha's first range was much larger than the ranges of homeless dogs reported in Baltimore by the behavioral scientist Alan Beck. Beck's urban strays had established tiny ranges of but 0.1 to 0.06 square mile. In contrast, Misha's range more closely resembled the 200- to 500-square-mile territories roamed by wolves, most notably the wolves reported by Adolph Murie in "The Wolves of Mount McKinley" and by L. David Mech in "The Wolves of Isle Royale." What was Misha doing?

Obviously, something unusual. Here was a dog who, despite his youth, could navigate flawlessly, finding his way to and from all corners of the city by day and by night. Here was a dog who could evade dangerous traffic and escape the dog officers and the dognappers who at the time supplied the flourishing laboratories of Cambridge with experimental animals. Here was a dog who never fell through the ice on the Charles River, a dog who never touched the poison baits set out by certain citizens for raccoons and other trash-marauders, a dog who never was mauled by other dogs. Misha always came back from his journeys feeling fine, ready for a light meal and a rest before going out again. How did he do it?

For a while I looked for the answer in journals and books, availing myself of the fine libraries at Harvard and reading everything I could about dogs to see if somewhere the light of science had penetrated this corner of dark. But I found nothing. Despite a vast array of publications on dogs, virtually nobody, neither scientist nor layman, had ever bothered to ask what dogs do when left to themselves. The few studies of free-ranging dogs concerned feral dogs, abandoned or homeless dogs. Alone in hostile settings, these forsaken creatures were surely under terrible stress. After all, they were not living under conditions that were natural to them, any more than are wild animals in captivity, imprisoned in laboratories and zoos. How might dogs conduct themselves if left undisturbed in normal circumstances? No one, apparently, had ever asked.

At first, that science had ignored the question seemed amazing. But was it really? We tend to study animals for what they can teach us about ourselves or for facts that we can turn to our advantage. Most of us have little interest in the aspects of their lives that do not involve us. But dogs? Dogs do involve us. They have shared our lives for twenty thousand years. How then had we managed to learn so little about dogs that we could not answer the simplest question: what do they want?

Our ignorance becomes more blameworthy when we consider that no animal could be easier to study. Unlike wild animals, dogs are not afraid of us. To study them we need not invade their habitat or imprison them in ours — our world *is* their natural habitat and always was. Furthermore, because their wild ancestors were not dogs at all but wolves, dogs have never even existed as a wild species. As a result we have had the opportunity to observe dogs since dogs began, an opportunity that for the most part we have chosen to ignore. Hence, curled on the sofa beside me of an evening was a creature of mystery: an agreeable dog with a life of his own, a life that he had no wish to conceal and that he was managing with all the competence of a wild animal, not with any help from human beings but in spite of them.

One evening he got up and stretched, preparatory to voyaging. First he braced his hind legs and stretched backward, head bowed, rump high, to pull tight the muscles of his shoulders. Then he raised his head and dropped his hips to stretch his spine and hind legs, even clenching his hind feet into fists so that the stretch went into his toes. Ready at last, he moved calmly toward the door so that, as usual, I could open it for him. And then, as our eyes met, I had an inspiration. Misha himself would answer my questions. Right in front of me, a long-neglected gate to the animal kingdom seemed waiting to be opened. Misha held the key.

Who could resist the appeal of this notion? No money, no travel, no training, no special instruments were necessary to probe the mystery — one needed only a dog, a notebook, and a pencil. I didn't even regret my total lack of formal training to begin such a project. In fact, because no biologists had ever hinted that they knew or even wondered what ordinary dogs want, my ignorance seemed almost a qualification. Anyway, I didn't feel I'd be ignorant for long. Turning out the lights so that the neighbors wouldn't see me flout the dog laws, at least not in this instance, I opened the door a crack. Out slipped Misha, with me right behind him, and thus our project began.

Again and again we did this, at least two or three nights a week for almost two years, not stopping even after Misha's owners came home to claim him, because by then Misha liked the work we were doing together and wanted to keep at it. Coming to collect me was not difficult for him — his community did not then have a leash law, so of an evening, after his owners let him out, he'd jump their fence and make his way across two cities to find me. Usually he would arrive after dark. By the light on our front porch I'd see him standing in the street, looking up at our windows like a captain looking for a sailor. I would turn out the porch light and crack the door, and Misha would slip inside for a brief visit with my family and also with his, for by then he had married my daughter's husky, the beautiful Maria, and was teaching some of his skills to the four children he had fathered on her. But eventually he would stand poised to go out again, looking back over his shoulder to see which of us would travel with him. Maria always volunteered, and if I wasn't going myself I'd sometimes let her. It was her or me, though, never both of us; if Maria and Misha were together, they traveled fast and wouldn't wait for me. Sometimes I took Maria on a leash, which kept us all together, but mostly I simply went alone with Misha. One by one, dog secrets were revealed through a series of adventures, some of them dangerous, all of them interesting. Misha was Odysseus, and Cambridge was the wine-dark sea.

THE FIRST question, perhaps the most important, perhaps even the most interesting, I was never able to answer. This was the question of Misha's navigational skills. To be sure, he had been traveling the streets of Cambridge long before I thought to go with him, and had probably memorized some landmarks. But sometimes he seemed to travel without the aid of landmarks, or at least not with the landmarks he had used to get where he was going, since once he had arrived at his destination, he might easily take another route home. Did he use the stars or the position of the sun? Did he see polarized light? Did he, like a carrier pigeon, hear the infrasound made by the Atlantic Ocean, so that he always knew which way was east? Did he use odors floating in the air, as fish use the taste of currents in seawater? I didn't know, and could learn nothing by watching his sure trot, his confident demeanor. To probe more deeply would have required an experiment — blindfolding him, say, and taking him to some distant release point. But that wasn't the nature of our relationship.

I did learn two things, though, about Misha's navigational ability. The first was that his skills were probably not innate, or not entirely so. If they had been, other huskies should have shared them. But I knew other Siberian huskies who could not navigate. One was Misha's wife, Maria. When they were together, Misha established the route for both of them, and not easily, because she, young and enthusiastic, would go bounding ahead of him, often in the wrong direction, requiring him to overtake her. Then, by jumping at her, he would literally have to knock her in the shoulder to try to make her turn. If after all his efforts she still wouldn't go where he wanted, he would resign himself to following her.

Many another dog would have obeyed her leader, but Maria had been a little spoiled by Misha, who encouraged her to do whatever she wanted, even when he knew that what she wanted was wrong. Of the two, he was unquestionably the stronger and could very easily have been dominant, but he was crazy about her. He let her do as she pleased, which seemed to delight her. As a result, though, Maria never learned to find her own way.

In this the dogs were like two people in a car, with the driver learning the route better and more easily than the passenger. And in later years, when Misha was no longer there to show the way, Maria invariably got lost when voyaging. Even when she went out with her adopted daughter, a dingo-spaniel cross named Fatima, who was an excellent navigator, they would get lost. Why? Because in the hierarchy of their group, Maria was at the very top, while Fatima, a generation below, was next to the bottom, and when Fatima traveled with Maria, Maria insisted on leading. Dominant but misinformed, Maria often bungled the job. But she wasn't stupid, even if she couldn't navigate. As soon as she realized she was lost, rather than turning to Fatima for a suggestion, she would simply sit down on someone's doorstep. Fatima would obediently sit down beside her, and eventually I would appear in a car to drive them home. Of course, the people whose house Maria had chosen would have read her identification tag and phoned me, but the particulars of my arrival didn't concern Maria. With her faithful daughter at her heels, she would clamber into the car like a tired shopper getting into a taxi, always to the puzzlement of her benefactors, who, assuming that a lost dog is a frightened dog, would be expecting her to rejoice profusely at the sight of me.

The second thing I learned about Misha's ability to navigate was that although he made his way faultlessly through the city, his technique didn't necessarily apply in the country, especially if he hadn't reached the starting point on his own. From my house in Cambridge, he and Maria sometimes traveled on their own as far as Concord, about twenty miles away, and would successfully find their way home a few days later, sometimes with deer hair in their stools. But if I took these dogs with me when I went to visit relatives in New Hampshire or on Nantucket, and if then the dogs went voyaging, Misha wasn't always able to lead Maria back to my relatives' home. Perhaps he felt less sure of himself in unfamiliar surroundings, and would surrender to her inept leadership. Whatever the reason, if both got lost in the country, they would use Maria's technique for getting home and wait on someone's doorstep for me to show up in the car.

*A*NOTHER VERY important skill of Misha's was his management of traffic. Cambridge suffers from some of the worst drivers in the nation, but no car as much as touched Misha, who, like a civil engineer, had divided the streets and their traffic into four categories and had developed different strategies to deal with each. The worst and most dangerous areas were congestions of multidirectional traffic, such as are found in Central, Porter, or Harvard Square. These areas Misha completely avoided. If he needed to be on the far side of one of them, he simply went around it. The second category was composed of a few limited-access highways, such as Alewife Parkway and Memorial Drive, where the heavy traffic of speeding cars was especially dangerous to dogs, not only because no legal or moral responsibility is attached to killing a dog, but also because dogs are down low, where motorists can't see them. Misha couldn't avoid the highways and still go where he wanted, so, adopting a humble attitude, he approached the cars with diplomacy and tact in an attempt to appease them.

Perhaps not surprisingly, many dogs treat cars as if they were animate. Dogs who chase cars evidently see them as large, unruly ungulates badly in need of discipline and shepherding, and can't help trying to control them. But Misha didn't chase cars. Being a husky and wearing very lightly the long domestication of his species, he felt no compulsion to assist mankind. However, he well understood that cars could be tremendously dangerous, especially when they seemed to be acting angrily and willfully, as they did on the limited-access highways. So he offered them respect. At the edge of the highway Misha would stand humbly, his head and tail low, his eyes half shut, his ears politely folded. If the cars could have seen him, they would have realized that he didn't challenge their authority.

But the moment the cars became few, Misha's humility would vanish. His ears would rise, his tail too, and he would bound fearlessly among them, the very picture of confidence. Over the highway he would skip, and go happily on his way. Never while I was observing him did I hear a scream of tires. Sometimes, though, he would lose me beside a limited-access highway. I lacked his courage, also his speed and skill, and I usually had to wait much longer than he did before the traffic conditions met my requirements for crossing. If traffic separated us, Misha would wait for a while on the far side, but sooner or later he would assume that I had lost interest and would travel on. Calling him back was out of the question for me — I couldn't have asked him to risk the traffic again on my behalf. Rather, if we became separated, I would simply go home. There he would find me waiting whenever his voyaging abated for a time.

Misha's third category of traffic included the main city streets. Cambridge's famous Brattle Street offers a perfect example, especially because Misha often used this street as a thoroughfare. Or rather, he used the sidewalk of Brattle Street as he traveled from one neighborhood to another, just as a human pedestrian would do. When crossing an intersecting street, however, Misha used a better and more intelligent method than his human counterparts. Unlike us, he didn't cross at the corner. Instead, he would turn up the intersecting street and go about twenty feet from the corner, cross there, and return on the sidewalk to Brattle Street's sidewalk, where he would continue his journey. At first I couldn't understand this maneuver, although Misha invariably used it. Then I saw its merits, and copied him thereafter. Why is Misha's method safer? Because at any point along the block, traffic comes from only two directions instead of from four directions, as it does at the intersection. By crossing at midblock, one reduces one's chances of being hit by a turning car. Since learning the midblock technique from Misha, I have noticed that almost all free-ranging dogs do likewise, as do people who need extra time to cross or who depend on their hearing for safety. Certain blind people, for instance, use the same technique.

Safety, however, was not Misha's only consideration. Usually, a tree or lamppost or mailbox or fire hydrant stands just behind the building line at the place where a traveling dog likes to cross the street. For dogs, the object serves the same function as a wayside inn at the ford of a river, a place that most travelers would visit of necessity, and therefore a good place to leave a message or a sign. Misha would visit these fixed objects, and after careful investigation would turn around and lift his leg. This is a very familiar sight to most dog owners. Virtually all male dogs mark permanent items (or what they believe to be permanent items) as they progress along a street. Sometimes Misha would mark repeatedly, passing a little urine, investigating his stain, and passing urine again, sometimes repeating the procedure as many as five or six times before he seemed satisfied and ready to carry on. Sometimes he rotated his body until his belly tilted upward, meanwhile standing on tiptoe to place his mark almost three feet above the ground. But even these very high stains did not always please him. If they weren't to his satisfaction, he would turn around and stretch even more, so that when he investigated, he would find his mark at his own eye level or higher.

What did it mean? Surely more than emptying the bladder. If Misha wanted merely to empty his bladder, he wouldn't bother to lift his leg at all but would bend his knees slightly, so as not to wet his hind feet, and release his urine, puppy-style, on the ground. Was Misha's leg-lifting an attempt to mark territory? That certainly was the popular explanation, an explanation that I had accepted as fact before my observation began. So I kept track of all the places Misha stained in order to learn what he felt he owned. Soon, though, I had an unwieldy sprawl of data that showed his alleged territory to be virtually everywhere he went. Was this possible? Wouldn't a dog as savvy as Misha want to discriminate to some degree between his home ground and distant places? Wouldn't he act one way in the place where he lived and another way in a distant area which he might visit only once? In fact, Misha's leg-lifting was about the same however far from home he happened to be.

In the residential streets, Misha's demeanor changed. Here he took no precaution about cars and never used a sidewalk, but instead moved daringly and purposefully up the middle of the street, eyes front, head and ears forward, tail up, the very picture of intent confidence. Even when he crossed an intersection, he did not alter his demeanor but kept scanning the street ahead. The trouble was that he couldn't see the cars speeding toward him on the cross street. Yet, amazingly, he always escaped them. How did he manage that?

I might never have learned if both his ears had been like the ears of most other huskies, stiff and upright. But they weren't. His left ear was soft at the tip, and when Misha was trotting along in a relaxed manner, the soft left tip bounced. When he was alert and tense, however, or when he noticed or thought of something important, the tip of his left ear would shoot up and stand stiff like the tip of his right ear. One day, while following Misha down a side street on the bike I had taken to using for my dogological studies, I saw his left ear stiffen as he approached an intersection. As was his custom, his eyes never left the street ahead, but the nearer he got to the intersection, the more his two ears stiffened and rotated outward, pointing sideways, so that by the time he was ready to cross, which he always did without changing his speed or shifting his gaze, the cups of his ears were pointing up and down the cross street. If a car was coming, he heard it. What was more, his hearing gave the speed of the car as well as its location, so that all Misha needed to do to avoid being hit was to pick up his pace or slow down, either to beat the car to the intersection or else to let it go across ahead of him. Scanning the street along which he was proceeding, never shifting his gaze to confirm what he heard coming from the sides, Misha would trot across the intersection smoothly, radiating coolness and self-confidence.

Why didn't he look at the cars? Because he was using his eyes to monitor the scene on the far side of the intersection. There, sensing Misha's approach, all the loose dogs of the neighborhood would leave their yards and porches and run out into the street.

And Misha wanted to be ready for them. He wanted to see them before they saw him, so he could prepare himself mentally for the meeting. Inevitably, the nearest dog would approach Misha with its tail and ears raised. When the approaching dog was about thirty feet away, Misha would slow his pace and advance more stiffly, his attention closely focused on the other dog, and gradually the two would come together.

Then Misha's neck would arch and his tail would rise. The other dog would stand still to meet him. Misha would approach stiffly and rapidly, and the two would stand slightly past each other, their heads by each other's necks. Misha usually averted his head to look sideways into the eye of the other dog, who usually looked directly but inquiringly at Misha and then averted his head slightly. Holding his tail high during these meetings, Misha kept his ears forward and the hair of his mantle slightly raised. If the other dog tried to investigate his groin or anus, Misha would leap sideways with his rear legs to avoid the investigation. Finally he would make his conclusive gesture: he would face the other dog's side with his neck highly arched and his nose pointing down almost into the other dog's hackles. Only after this would he sometimes switch his stance again and let the other dog investigate him.

Everyone has watched such a meeting. Sometimes just as the tension seems to be relaxing, one dog knocks the other with his hips. Sometimes the second dog does not react visibly and the circling goes on, but sometimes the second dog staggers slightly, then folds his ears and lowers his tail a bit. No person knows exactly what the hip test tells the participants, but probably the dogs have felt each other's mass. At any rate, the test seems to help them reach an agreement. They usually separate soon afterward, each going his own way. Very inconspicuously, Misha would administer the hip test to every dog who cared to encounter him, and invariably emerged from the encounter with his tail high, a sign of his transcendence over the other dog, who emerged with his tail low. Then Misha might invite or be invited by the other dog to play, and the two might frisk briefly. Misha might invite the other dog to follow him, which he did by trotting onward, looking back at the other dog meanwhile.

Always pragmatic, Misha never bothered to circle tiny dogs, but just swept by them or stepped over them, and he never tried to circle huge dogs, whom he pretended to ignore. Anyone would know that he was superior to the tiny dogs, and evidently he didn't want anyone to notice that the huge dogs could have been physically superior to him. Instead, he concentrated on dogs within ten or fifteen pounds of his own size (a size range that probably included more than 90 percent of the dogs he encountered) and circled to establish his superiority to them. He spent more time circling the male dogs than the female dogs, who tended to be less forthcoming, often circling Misha only long enough to learn his sex and attitude before backing off. Whatever the sex of his challenger, though, the moment the encounter ended, Misha, with his supremacy intact, would continue up the street to repeat exactly the same behavior with every dog who didn't retreat from him. On and on he traveled, in long straight lines about the city, concluding his business in one residential neighborhood only to penetrate another, where once again, radiating coolness, he would circle all comers.

At first I saw these dog encounters as yet another obstacle to Misha's travels, something like the problems of navigation and of traffic, problems to solve in order to reach his goal. So I followed him patiently from neighborhood to neighborhood, growing increasingly puzzled that he never seemed to find what he sought. I had already decided that he wasn't looking for companionship — he never spent more than a minute with a local dog, and anyway, he had his own group at our house, his loyal wife and children and two other dogs, both pugs, who, because of their small size, had from the start been his subordinates and would heel to him when we all went walking together. (To do this I had only to keep Misha's wife, Maria, on a leash so that she and he couldn't run away together.) I also felt sure that Misha's voyaging wasn't a search for sex, mainly because few if any estrous females were available. Stray dogs stigmatize a neighborhood, and the Cantabridgians, exquisitely sensitive to status, didn't tolerate stigmata well, especially not the jovial crowds of male dogs that inevitably gather to mill outside the house of a female in season, relentlessly marking with urine all the bushes and buildings and mounting people's legs. Occasionally in my travels with Misha I would see a crowd of milling males, but the female who had lured them was never in evidence. Realistic Misha seldom joined the crowd, or not for long. And never while I was traveling with him did he encounter a female he could, as it were, put his leg over.

Finally, having ruled out companionship and sex as Misha's motives for voyaging, I also ruled out food and hunting. At home I offered him plenty to eat, yet he always ate sparingly, and other people's food didn't tempt him. Nor did he overturn garbage

cans or care about their contents. Rather, he investigated only the outer surfaces of garbage cans, probably because they had been marked by other dogs.
Odoriferous, food-related trash such as fast-food
wrappers held little interest for him. And he all but
ignored the live suburban prey species, such as cats
and small wild mammals. Even squirrels, which
most dogs seem unable to resist chasing, Misha
coursed very lightly. No sooner had he gotten a
squirrel started up a tree than he would abandon
it to return to his voyaging, penetrating ever more
Cambridge neighborhoods and circling ever more
dogs. At last I reached the inescapable conclusion
that to circle other dogs was not merely a byproduct
of Misha's questing. To circle other dogs was his
purpose.

THE CONCLUSION was disappointing. My lengthy and painstaking observations of someone else's husky, an animal whose free-ranging behavior had made my name known in police stations throughout the Greater Boston area, seemed suddenly like peeling an onion. Evidently my efforts were gaining me nothing more than I could have seen by glancing out a window. No hunts? No joining wild packs? "Is this all?" I asked Misha one night with some irritation as my bicycle wobbled behind his pale hindquarters down yet another darkened residential street. Misha heard me. Deviating from his normal eyes-front demeanor, he looked back pleasantly over his shoulder to give me a glance, quick and frank.

So I continued to follow him through the autumn and winter, until a big storm buried Cambridge in snow, so that the trees were plastered in white and the snowbanks rose higher than people's heads. Then I could see what before had been invisible, the footprints and the urine stains of other dogs. Apparently Misha was not the only one who used the midblock method for crossing big streets. The tracks of other dogs revealed that those who were not under the physical control of a person used the midblock method too, whether or not a scent-marked object such as a tree or a fire hydrant was present to lure them. If such a marking post was present, the dogs predictably went to it. Not so predictable was what they actually did there, which was not merely to leave their own stains — an end in itself if the goal was simply to claim territory — but to investigate and overmark the stains of others. And then I noticed that when Misha marked the same place a second or third time, he did so because a particle of another dog's stain remained uncovered. Only when the underlying stain seemed completely obliterated did Misha appear satisfied and ready to move on.

But why? One day, while watching Misha nearly invert himself to place an extremely high stain on a snowbank near our door, I found myself idly thinking that any dog who could make such a stain by a normal tilt of his leg would have to be a giant. And suddenly it hit me. Perhaps that was the point! Perhaps Misha wanted to give the impression that he who had made the stain was a giant. The more I thought about this explanation, the better it seemed. In fact, making the right impression seemed to be Misha's entire strategy.

Just how serious Misha was about his image was brought home to me one afternoon on a main street, after he had managed to pass through the rush-hour traffic on a limited-access highway but I had not. I had turned back and was leaving the area when I noticed a Saint Bernard. This huge dog was well known to the neighborhood for ferociously de-

The dog became suspicious as we passed his yard, and when I unexpectedly turned back, he came out into the street. There he barked a challenge, making me wonder how I would get by him, since he commanded the entire street and both sidewalks. Meanwhile, Misha had noticed my absence and had once again breasted the river of highway traffic to return to me. As he reappeared from the torrent of cars, the Saint Bernard saw him and began barking furiously. How could Misha go by him without changing course, or scurrying, or bolting, or otherwise seeming to come off second best and thus losing face? He couldn't turn back, because the Saint Bernard might decide to chase him, forcing him into the dangerous traffic. Nor could he keep trotting down the street into the Saint Bernard's space, where, when attacked, he would have to break into an undignified run, not at all cool but hurried and scampering.

For a few seconds things looked bad for Misha. But then he solved the problem brilliantly. Head up, tail loosely high like a banner of self-confidence, he broke into a canter and bounded straight for the Saint Bernard, but without looking at him. Before anyone realized what had happened, Misha was soaring by, his eyes on something far away, as if he didn't realize the Saint Bernard was there. If the monster at that point had decided to attack, Misha would have been already in motion, and as he was much faster than the giant, he could have sped away without seeming to flee. But apparently everything happened so fast that the Saint Bernard felt bewildered. His barking became louder and faster after

Misha was past, as if he thought he had failed to get Misha's attention in the first place.

Much has been written about demeanor, especially the demeanor of prey animals when confronted by predators. For instance, an observer in Canada described the behavior of five bison, three healthy and two sick, who were resting in the open when some wolves appeared. At the approach of the wolves, the two sick bison, knowing they were vulnerable, hastily got to their feet, while the three healthy bison, feeling confident, stayed put. The implication of such behavior was not lost on the wolves, who promptly chose one of the sick bison and killed her. Thus, the importance of demeanor cannot be overemphasized, and is widely understood.

I remember the demeanor of a yearling wolf I saw on Baffin Island, where, in the company of four Canadian biologists sent to survey the caribou, I went to visit the wolves. The part of Baffin we visited was not mapped in much detail. We walked to the study area from a DEW Line station, about seventy-five miles over the tundra. Since no human beings have ever lived inland on Baffin, most of the animals didn't know what we were. The wolf in question was startled to see us when, rounding the edge of a hill, he and his mother came upon us resting by a trail. Both wolves seemed surprised by the sight, and the mother streaked off toward the horizon. The youngster, however, was more naive, and not knowing how to behave in such unexpected circumstances, he acted more traditionally. Rather than risk stimulating our predatory instincts by running from us, he chose to appear normal and cool, and he continued trotting as though he knew of nothing wrong. Soon, though, he trotted into the territory of a nesting jaeger, who took to the air and began to dive fiercely at his head. I actually heard the blows her sharp beak gave him. But the youngster was so committed to his display of calm that he couldn't respond. Without as much as a whimper, he jogged determinedly onward while the bird dove repeatedly upon him, biting him so hard that his skin and fur flew. Only when he thought himself far enough away from us that sudden movement on his part wouldn't bring one of us dashing after him did he feel able to deal with the jaeger. But then, changing instantly from a milquetoast to a demon, he hurled himself into the air and almost caught her. Astonished, she flapped and squawked, lost a feather, then gained altitude and flew back to her nest while the young wolf ran after his mother.

Misha understood the importance of a cool demeanor and so did the young wolf, but Misha's adversary, the big Saint Bernard, did not. His passion and intensity on behalf of his owners eventually proved too much for them, and they took him to the local humane society. Supposedly, he was offered for adoption. But most people don't want a huge dog with very strong feelings. No one took him. That humane society was also a dog hospital, where a dog's emergency later took me, and there, to my surprise, I recognized the Saint Bernard, who was standing helplessly in a little wire cage. Our eyes met. His face brightened, because, I think, he recognized me. I saw that he very much hoped I would help him, but alas, I could not. Scheduled for execution, he was waiting to be drained of blood to provide transfusions for dogs more fortunate than he, dogs who were wanted by their owners.

WHY DOES a dog need high rank? Among dogs as among people, there are many reasons. To a wild animal, especially a social animal, high rank can mean life, not only for the animal itself but also for its children. Among the wild canids and even among free-ranging domestic dogs, males of high rank are more likely than not to be selected for mating by females, while the rank of a female can make the difference between life and death for her children. Wolves know this, and dogs who are free to make their own choices show that they know it too.

When I went to Baffin Island, which I did during the time Misha was showing me dog life in the streets of Cambridge, I felt sure I would see the drama of canid survival enacted in its highest form. What I actually saw was a lonely group of five adult wolves working very hard to feed seven hungry pups. They seemed to be a family, probably a mother and father with three yearling children who were helping their parents to care for the little ones. The wolves maintained a series of five dens on hills along a river system, as wolves will, often occupying a different den each year, conceivably as a method of flea control. That year they were in the fourth in line, traveling west to east. I found myself a small, shallow cave on a nearby hill where I camped alone to observe the wolves.

One of the first things I noticed was a system of trails, their trails, that led from the hill out across the vast surrounding tundra, and one day, while following the wolves' main east-west trail, I came upon something so inconspicuous and seemingly trivial that I almost missed it: the trail became a shallow groove as it crossed a ledge of rock. That wolves had worn the groove was irrefutable; the trail led straight to the mouth of the den, and thus was not a route that other animals would have chosen. Anyway, there were almost no other animals who could have made such a trail. Birds, a few insects, hares, foxes, lemmings, and voles are the only animals besides wolves and caribou who live inland on Baffin. Polar bears and people seldom venture inland from the coast. More significant, though, was the fact that the ledge extended only a few inches from the vertical surface of a lofty formation of rock that rose straight up from a lake and made the trail at that point much too narrow for me or any other wide animal to use without falling into the icy water. Thus, the ledge would have been much too narrow for caribou, who are the only creatures on Baffin other than wolves to make trails of any significance. Furthermore, because the ledge was uneven, much of the trail was slightly under water. At first this was what struck me about it. I could envision a wolf ankle-deep in water, splashing along. But slowly the true importance of the groove dawned on me, until I realized I might be seeing one of the most important sights that I would ever see. On a mountain near my home, booted hikers by the thousands had used a trail across a granite slab for over a century without noticeably marking it. How long before the booted hikers would wear a groove? And what if the trail were used only by wolves? And by only five or six wolves each year? And used only a few times a week and only in summer, and with feet touching rock only when the trail and the lake were free of ice and snow? One doesn't often see very old things made by animals. I realized that I was looking at one of them.

Also ancient, it seems, was the use of the den site. Surely the hole itself had been redug from time to time, but certainly the wolves' occupancy of the hill was old. How old? Thousands of years? Long ago, big white wolves had moved to Baffin from the mainland and begat the island subspecies — a new race of small white wolves. Had the early pioneers found the hill and settled on it? Possibly so. Year after year wolves had taken the same route to the hill, because it was the best route, the easiest way, leading around bogs wherever possible, crossing ridges at their lowest points. Each refinement of the route saved energy. But why was that particular hill so desirable that wolves had been walking to it long enough to wear a groove in the rock? And who were these wolves?

In fact, the hill had everything a wolf could want in a den site. Located about halfway between the summer grounds and winter grounds of a herd of caribou, the den was always within a few days' travel of good hunting. Better yet, in spring, when the pups were born and their mother stayed in the den to feed and warm them, the caribou, accompanied by fawns, were passing right by the hill on their way to their summer pasture. And in the fall, when the wolf pups were gangling adolescents with ravenous appetites, when they needed more food than ever before but couldn't yet help with the hunting, the caribou, fattened up for winter, were migrating right past the den again, going back to their calving grounds. Yet the hunting opportunities were not the only advantages of the hill. Seemingly the deposit of a glacier, its soil was sandy enough to dig but also firm enough to hold a shape, so the wolves could dig a den that would not collapse on them.

The hill was also an excellent lookout. In the center of a vast basin ringed by higher hills, it commanded a 360-degree view for many miles in all directions, and was bordered on the south side by a stream. The latter was particularly important, not only because denning wolves need water to drink yet cannot provision one another with water as they can with food, but also because the stream served as a fence. For their own safety, the seven pups were supposed to stay at the den, but there they would get lonely and would inevitably try to follow a departing adult. Naturally, the adults couldn't let this happen — the pups would slow them down and spoil their hunting — so they would leave by heading south, at least to start with, and would jump over the stream, which was so wide and so deep that the pups couldn't follow. And the water was so cold they wouldn't try to swim. Instead, they would stand on the bank, forlorn and crying, watching the adults, who were obviously torn between going and staying, as they reluctantly trotted away.

Thus, the question of why that particular hill had been chosen as a den site was easy to answer. Any wolf would want such a place. Furthermore, because few places in the world are so perfect, most wolves must make do with much less. Who, therefore, were the wolves who lived there, and why were they, and not some other wolves, the occupants? Wolves are well known to be territorial, which is to say that they lay claim to certain areas, which they defend as best they can from other wolves. Whatever wolves owned the den site wouldn't willingly share it with strange wolves. This alone would tend to keep a den site in a family, all the more so because wolves, like most birds and many other mammals, apparently prefer ancestral nesting places. But were the current occupants of the den descendants of the first settlers? Could a den have been occupied by the same family for several thousand years? Although theoretically anything is possible, such long tenure would be unlikely. Probably the excellent site changed hands from time to time. I came to see it as resembling a medieval fort, a castle, remote and isolated, with a little band of occupants, probably an extended family, who spent most of their days simply putting food on the table yet who stood ready to repel invaders and whose ownership could be traced back in time, even a long time, to a heroic ancestor who had built the castle or had wrested it from its previous occupants. Ownership had been handed from parent to child; the primogeniture of human beings is, after all, little more than favoring the dominant child. The more I thought about it, the more the ancient landed gentry of Europe came to seem like wolves, with one pair, the dominant male and female, owning a territory and the castles upon it and hunting the deer for miles around. Dominance and ownership were surely very closely tied.

This, obviously, is still true of wolves. For them, ownership of a den is crucial, since without a sheltering den a pack disintegrates. Adult wolves don't need dens; adults can withstand terrible exposure. But their infants cannot. Like human infants, wolf pups can barely keep themselves warm, let alone survive outdoors in an Arctic winter. Furthermore, since wolves must be almost full-grown to have any hope of surviving the first winter, which is the greatest killer of young wolves, they must be born as early in the year as possible so they have time to grow. To this end, wolves mate in February and bear their pups in March, long before the snow melts. Dens cannot be dug in the frozen earth, so a pair of wolves without a den will surely lose their pups to the weather. And in any group of wolves, no matter who is pregnant, the dominant female gets to give birth inside the den. Thus ownership and dominance are life itself to wolves, and dogs remember this, and act accordingly. The old memory partly explains why Misha liked to circle other dogs.

As for the wolves, around their ancient homestead lay a vast and empty tundra where, because the Arctic plants were small and ground-hugging, nothing resisted the wind. The wind would push the clouds or turn the wolves' fur but make no sound. In this lonely silence, under the radiant Arctic sun, the five adult wolves assumed their responsibilities with competence and skill, so seasoned by hard work and so accustomed to one another that they interacted rarely, if at all. There were no dominance displays among these lonely toilers — in the way of all close families, they well knew who was who without reminding one another. And anyway, like a hard-working farm family or a lonely band of hunter-gatherers, the wolves had little time for anything but winning their livelihood from an unforgiving world.

Traveling singly or in pairs, four of them at any given time would almost always be hunting far away, while the fifth stayed at the den to babysit, often so tired that he or she would spend the entire time sleeping high on a ledge, out of reach of the pestering youngsters. For a while the pups would try to reach the babysitter, but eventually they would give up, fall silent, realize that everyone had gone and that the sitter wouldn't play with them, wait a few minutes longer, as if hoping they'd been mistaken, but at last creep inside the den. Yet not to forget about the outside world — the moment a hunter returned, bringing food, the pups would rush out and mob him. Quickly the returning wolf would lower his head, arch his back, heave his stomach, and lay out a pile of chopped meat, which the puppies would gobble instantly, literally in a second or two; then they would rush after the retreating newcomer, crying, crowding, kissing, pleading for more.

Once or twice during my time of observation, the pups' mother, who was the highest-ranking female, actually gave more, lowering her head to produce a second, smaller pile, probably food she had planned to keep for herself. But usually after giving up one generous serving, the newcomer would simply trade places with the babysitter. Then the footsore newcomer would curl up on the ledge out of reach of the puppies, while the erstwhile babysitter would stretch and shake, nose here or there as if procrastinating, pass some urine, squeeze out a scat, drink a sip of water from the nearby stream, and perhaps stand around thinking for a minute or two, possibly trying to decide on a direction. Sooner or later she would choose one of the paths in the web of wolf trails, and trudging slowly at first, as if her mind were weighted with the enormity of the task ahead, then gradually picking up her pace, as if resigning herself to her work, she would at last settle into the businesslike, ground-covering trot of a wolf with a far destination, a wolf who once again sets out to do her best and won't waste time pitying herself because she must do it. By then the new babysitter would be fast in an exhausted sleep, and would stay asleep until another wolf returned from the field to replace him. Because there is no darkness in high summer on Baffin, I could watch around the clock, and once watched a tired wolf sleep for eighteen hours straight, from the time he bedded down on the babysitter's ledge until his replacement arrived and he went hunting again. After his first nine hours of motionless sleep, he raised his head, sighed, opened and shut his mouth to settle his tongue, and went back to sleep for nine more hours. Thus toil and sleep made up life as it was led by the rustic wolves of Baffin.

It became my impression that as boring as so provincial and mundane a life might seem to modern urban people, the wolves liked it. The orderly life, the daily routine, and the silent tundra in its annual gyre around the sun may have offered welcome predictability to those caribou hunters, each of whom was obliged, every few days, to travel a great distance alone, first to search for a likely victim, then to close in on it, then, if possible, to attack it, and finally to bring it down. An adult Baffin wolf is less than half the size of an adult Baffin caribou, and caribou are virtually the only large prey on the island. But they are not easy prey, especially since both sexes have antlers, and especially not for wolves, who have no claws with which to seize them, let alone guns, spears, or arrows with which to kill them from afar.

In fact, caribou hunting is so difficult that most people, who might feel too timid even to walk up to and stroke a large ungulate, especially a wild one, find an actual capture hard to visualize. If you are a wolf, though, even if you feel as timid as a person, you must nevertheless put your face right against the neck and into the fur of a huge, terrified animal with feet like flying hammers, an animal that bites and kicks and hates you, and you must kill it with your mouth. To come back unscathed, especially with a full stomach, is in itself a success story, and may explain why wolves seem to want mundane, orderly lives when not hunting.

When I visited Baffin with the Canadian scientists, our appearance on the river system came as a puzzling and perhaps unwelcome surprise to the wolves who lived there. The young wolf and his mother were the first to see us, and upon their reunion after the youngster's adventure with the jaeger, they evidently went straight back to the den, where they howled. Apparently they called the others in from the field, because about an hour later they all howled together, a chorus of haunting voices that rose and fell, perhaps to express their solidarity vis-à-vis our group, or perhaps to tell us that the river system was owned by them and that we should move. The wolf call starts low, rises quickly, and falls slowly, and lends itself to choral singing in that the next voice can join at any one of several points, so that the effect is polyphonic, like a round. Wolves like to howl together; their faces and eager mannerisms before and after howling show this. I believe the experience intensifies their positive feelings for one another. It does for us. And as we sing communally to heighten team spirit before important competitions such as sporting events or battles, so do wolves.

When we heard them, one of the scientists, whose name was Clive Elliott, said in effect that the wolves had called an assembly because we had appeared, and furthermore that it would soon seem to us as if the mother and son had called in the others to warn them away from us. This proved true. Uncanny as it seems, as long as we stayed there, the wolves never again visited the place where they first spotted us, the place that became our main camp, even though we certainly didn't threaten them but instead put out very odoriferous baits to lure them. They later tolerated and even visited me in my camp right by their den, and a wolverine came gladly enough to eat the baits, but as Clive foresaw, the wolves thereafter avoided our main camp, just as if the two who had seen us told the others where a surprising and untoward thing had occurred. In fact, they almost certainly had done just that. None of us knew how they managed the communication, but then, wolf communication is merely one of many things about animals that people don't fully understand.

*I*N CONTRAST to the wolves of Baffin, my dogs at home led lives of high drama whether they wanted to or not. This is the fate of city dogs when several of them live together, free to do more or less as they please, especially if they are not all re-lated and if their group interacts from time to time with neighboring dogs. Unlike the seemingly isolated wolf family of Baffin, whose status vis-à-vis one another seemed firmly established, my dogs spent much of their time and energy trying to rearrange their hierarchy, probably because of the way their group had been composed. If the wolves were an actual family, a mother, father, grown children, and infants, some of the dogs were little more than friends, and, at least at first, lacked a deep commitment to one another.

Their group began simply enough, with a young male pug named Bingo. A confident little creature, Bingo was much admired, and he knew it. "You're a big little dog," my father would say to him fondly. Bingo would reward my father by placing his front feet on my father's kneecaps and looking up into his face. One day Bingo ran in front of a car, was hit, and lost an eye. At the hospital he so ingratiated himself through his courage and his friendly, forthright ways that the veterinarian offered to buy him. But we loved Bingo and didn't want to part with him.

Probably we would have gone on living with him as the only dog in the family, unaware of the rich drama that dogs in groups might enact before our eyes, had we not decided that we had been unfair in having a boy dog for our son but not a girl dog for our daughter, and acquired another pug, a female with impressive registration papers, bred for show. Poor little creature, she soon grew up to be a dithering, hyperexcited adult, whose frequent episodes of panic were probably caused by the fact that during exertion she would have so much difficulty breathing that she would almost black out. This, we learned, is common in toy breeds with gruesomely foreshortened faces. Born with the same number of sinuses and teeth, the same amount of tongue, soft palate, and nasal passages as normal dogs, they lack the proper space to house these organs: all are squashed together inside the deformed skull. Violet (for so our daughter named the little female) was more highly bred and more deformed than Bingo. And unfortunately, she wasn't as smart. She couldn't remember or didn't understand, for instance, that strenuous exercise would cause her to gasp for breath and even to collapse in a convulsion, so she collapsed a lot. Nor could she learn the usual canine skills. We considered it a triumph to housebreak her even partially. She was oblivious to her surroundings, could never be let off a leash, and once, mistaking duckweed on a pond for grass, ran off the end of a dock and almost drowned.

Seeing how unsuited she was for almost any activity except exhibition at a dog show, numerous people suggested that we find another home for Violet. But she wouldn't have liked that. Her heart was in our house, and her condition didn't limit her capacity for affection, which was enormous. Yet the object of her affection was not any one of us; although we fed and loved her and let her sleep on the beds, she gave us merely her wan good will, while reserving her deeper feelings for Bingo. From the moment she set eyes on him, she adored him. Wanting only to be near him, to lavish her affection on him, she followed everywhere he went. The sound of his voice made her bark.

Bingo's affection for Violet was less than hers for him. Even so, he depended on her. Like two little married people, they had their private arrangements — a way they liked to sleep, an agreement that she would relinquish her food to him if he finished his food first, an ongoing struggle about her walking ahead of him on his blind side, forcing him to shoulder her back. Like a little married man, Bingo saw as his duty getting both himself and Violet into the house if they were outside, and to this end he would stand on his hind legs and vigorously scratch the wooden door. He worked so hard that he dug deep furrows, some of which nearly penetrated the panels. Violet always sat right beside him, watching uneasily.

Because of Violet's physical inadequacies, she was not much of a canine companion, especially for a child. When Bingo was three and Violet was two, we realized that we had not done our daughter any favor. So Violet became my dog, and for our daughter we found and adopted a third dog, the beautiful young husky Maria.

Healthy and athletic, Maria was everything that Violet was not. Bingo immediately became deeply interested in her. As the eldest and therefore the dominant dog of the household, he would demonstrate in front of her, walking slowly and stiffly back and forth across her path, but with his ears held low and his face radiating affection. His body language told her that he knew she was younger than he, and furthermore that she was his junior as a member of the household, so he was her superior in every way that mattered to dogs, but all that was as nothing, since he already felt much affection for her and wanted her to be his follower and his lady.

Quiet young Maria watched all this with a certain reserve. She was new to the house, it was true, but she had spent her first five months of life with both her parents as well as her siblings and her father's brother, and as a result of having been so highly socialized to dogs, she had excellent canine manners and knew just how to behave herself. With her tail low but her ears alert, she seemed to draw into herself a little, letting her demeanor show only partial submission — enough for a start. She meant that she was willing to respect Bingo but would await developments to see what the nature of their future relationship might be. Dogs, after all, don't automatically bond just because they share houseroom. Rather, many if not most dogs who live together arrive at a relationship resembling that of siblings or of coworkers in an office: they establish rank immediately, but after that they are often content merely to avoid disputes. When tasks arise, such as warning of intruders or driving off other dogs, the housemates usually cooperate, and often they travel or hunt together, especially if they live in the country. But such cooperation merely means that the relationship is amiable, nothing more.

In contrast to Bingo, Violet made no effort to establish her rank. Instead, she seemed unable to come to grips with the problem of Maria. It was true that Maria was vastly stronger and more energetic than Violet, and had long, glistening white teeth, the teeth of an early or primitive dog, not Violet's sorry, twisted little pegs, which are all that are left to a hapless pug after centuries of pitiless domestication. Even so, in many households a small elderly dog easily dominates a large young newcomer by sheer force of personality, and Violet might have been better off if she had tried for some psychological ascendancy over Maria while Maria was still young. The void that resulted from Violet's failure became an invitation for Maria to play with her like a cat with a mouse, like a child with a toy, and poor, besieged little Violet would then rush at Maria in a passion, snarling and gasping and trying to bite. Maria, seeming to misinterpret Violet's desperation, would dance around her joyfully until a human being would remove one of them from the scene.

What bothered Violet most about Maria, though, was that Bingo liked her so much. Ignoring Violet, Bingo spent time every day trying to make a conquest of Maria by parading back and forth beside her with his ears low, his expression soft, and his tail very faintly wagging. Violet often tried to stop him. She would rush him, yapping and jumping at him so that her chest bumped hard against his shoulder, as if she were trying to knock him aside, out of the way. He would turn and snarl suddenly, then resume his pleasant face. He couldn't sustain anger for very long lest Maria misunderstand him and think that she was its object, but even the flash was enough for Violet, who by then was too low in the hierarchy even to think of challenging Maria directly, and would withdraw to a distant corner and sit down, chastened and depressed.

The issue reached a climax when Maria was a year old and showed signs of coming into her second heat. Bingo was transported. Redoubling his efforts, he would follow wherever she went and, touchingly enough, would actually walk on tiptoes, perhaps to make himself seem taller. Maria seemed to feel almost stifled by his attention. Usually she tried to ignore him, but when he made this impossible by his importuning, she would give him a hard glance and leave, sometimes leaping onto the sofa and curling herself into a tight ball, from which position she would stare at the world with angry eyes. Evidently she had no thought of holding her tail aside for Bingo.

Do dogs have morals? Bingo did. Under the circumstances, given his adoration of Maria, he should by nature have wanted to do everything to please her. Yet one night he defied her in order to accomplish what he thought was right. Even though the account of his deed reveals my own shameful behavior, I offer it here because I find it both mysterious and extraordinary.

We had in our kitchen an immense partitioned cage in which our children kept two parakeets and three white mice. For weeks Maria had ignored the little captives, but late one night, as she was passing through the dimly lit kitchen, she evidently noticed them for the first time and lunged at a parakeet sportingly. Of course it flew, startling the mice and the other parakeet, and soon Maria was tearing around the cage in a frenzy, trying to catch the panicky creatures flapping and scurrying inside. I should have stopped her immediately. But since she couldn't really hurt the captives, only scare them, and because I was so fascinated by her total lack of aggression, her joyous sense of the chase, I kept watching, and despite my conscience let the terror go on and on.

But suddenly something struck Maria's side so hard that she yelped and stumbled. It was Bingo, who had come unnoticed into the kitchen and now planted himself between the astonished Maria and the cage. She recovered at once, and ignoring Bingo, she rushed the cage again. But Bingo barked with great authority, a shout of a bark, and again he slammed himself into Maria. Amazed, she stopped, and then, as dogs will when circumstances seem too puzzling, she simply left the scene, withdrawing to the far side of the room to see what would happen next. There she stayed. Then all of us were quiet in the half-lit room, Bingo trembling with emotion and panting hard as he faced Maria watchfully, Maria overwhelmed by this unexpected turn of events, me shamed by my own dog, and the mice and the parakeets exhausted and still. Bingo stayed where he was as guardian until Maria left the room. Then I reached my hand to him apologetically. Quietly, humbly, he touched my fingers very delicately with his tongue.

What had happened? Had Bingo come to the defense of the helpless mice and birds? Possibly, I suppose, but there are better explanations. He may, for instance, have seen the mice and parakeets in the way that larger dogs see farm animals, as the chattel of their masters, in need of protection. Or perhaps he saw Maria's high excitement as a situation gone haywire and wanted to bring the household back under control. Whatever his interpretation, though, his deed speaks well for the strength of his moral fiber. The fact is, male dogs in love tend to let their females do just about anything, but Bingo stopped Maria from acting in a way he thought was wrong.

*A*T ABOUT this time, a fourth dog entered the picture. This dog was Misha, whose owners brought him to our house for a preliminary visit, to get him used to his new quarters before they left for Europe. He burst through the front door ahead of them, straining at his leash. We released him just as Maria came out of the kitchen, and just as Bingo came swaggering down the stairs to see who was at the door. Bingo's usual role on such an occasion was to bark rigorously until the visiting person had been admitted, then to place his front feet against the visitor's knees in greeting or acceptance, then, with head and tail high, to walk slowly ahead of the visitor, as if leading him or her into the house. Prepared to do the same this time, Bingo stopped in his tracks at the sight of Misha, the big stranger, and then began to advance in a threatening manner.

But Misha barely noticed Bingo. His eyes had met Maria's. Over Bingo's head he bounded, to skid to a stop in front of Maria, who at once dropped to her elbows in an invitation to play. *Chase me,* her gesture said. And he did. Quickly, lightly, the two delighted creatures spun away around the room, jumping from the sofa to the chair to the windowseat to the table and over the sofa again, all in perfect silence except for the furniture scraping as they pushed it and now and then the crash of a book or other object accidentally knocked over. Their feet seldom touched the floor. With their shining eyes and bursting energy, the two dogs in their happiness were one of the loveliest sights I had ever seen. I could have watched forever.

Meanwhile, Bingo was trying to make himself felt. He would have liked to stalk slowly back and forth in front of Misha while staring up at him, a display of superior status, but because Bingo was down on the floor while Misha was leaping over the furniture in pursuit of the elegant Maria, Bingo's display went unnoticed. When Misha didn't even see Bingo, Bingo increased his threats. Throwing himself in Misha's path as Misha ricocheted briefly off the sofa, Bingo tried to bite Misha's leg. But Misha was only touching down; as he flew up again, he accidentally knocked Bingo over. With a roar, Bingo ran after him. Suddenly remembering ourselves in the midst of the two feathery, flying beauties, we ran after Bingo, caught him, and put him in another room. Misha and Maria were so taken with each other that they noticed nothing. Misha didn't even notice when his owners left.

About a week after their first meeting, Maria felt ready to mate. Planting her feet very firmly and looking affectionately over her shoulder at Misha, she swept her tail aside until it almost lay along her body. Misha mounted, throwing his foreleg over her back. They joined. A virgin, she yelped once, but didn't struggle. Soon they locked, and then, with their ears folded and their faces gentle and smiling, with their mouths open and with their breathing rapid as their body temperature soared, they turned rump to rump and sank to the floor. After a long time they came apart, then turned to each other, began to kiss, and then to frisk around the room. The door to the yard was open. Out they ran, to race each other joyfully. To his credit, Bingo, who

was present, rejoiced with them in spirit. His face
soft, he kept glancing at us lovingly, as if to invite
our approval of the great event. But for the most
part he kept to the far side of the room, away from
Misha and Maria, approaching them only once or
twice, gently happy (as many dogs are in the presence of a mating pair) but not expectant, not even
very hopeful of getting a turn.

He was right not to hope, since Maria had never
encouraged him. Nor did she ever receive him, unlike many female dogs, who give themselves either
to more than one male at a session or to different
males on different days, with the result that the pups
of one litter have different fathers. So carefully did
Maria save herself for Misha that when she went
outside to urinate she didn't mark, as female dogs in
estrus often do by squatting partway down, raising a
leg, and directing their urine to the base of some
large wayside object such as a tree so that the scent
can be carried far and wide on the feet of passersby.
In later years, when she no longer had Misha, she
advertised her sexual condition. And in later years
she showed a willingness to accept other dogs (but
never Bingo).

From the day they met, Misha and Maria ate together, went out together, and slept together fur to

fur. When Misha's owners came to take him home from his preliminary visit, they had to drag him, and in an hour he was back, having jumped their fence. He then released Maria from our yard, which he did by tunneling underneath the fence, and she became his companion in voyaging. They would be gone all day, and often all night too, and I'd find them curled on the front steps in the morning. When we were forced to prevent Maria from traveling, because of the leash law, she would wait near the door for her husband, and when he came in she would approach him swiftly and bury her nose in his mantle while he stood still, waiting patiently while she investigated him. This, of course, is why dogs roll on things. Social creatures that they are, they wear the odors home and share the information. From that time onward, Misha's home was with Maria, as was hers with him. To her he would return from voyaging, if we hadn't let her join him. While he was away she would wait for him, sitting by the door or looking out a window. When she saw him she'd jump up, so we knew to open the door and let him in. Popular prejudice might hold that romantic love, with its resulting benefit of fidelity, sexual and otherwise, is not a concept that can be applied to dogs, and that to do so is anthropomorphic. Not true. Fully as much as any human love story, the story of Misha and Maria shows the evolutionary value of romantic love. The force that drove Romeo and Juliet is no less strong or important if harbored by a nonhuman species, because the strength of the bond helps to assure the male that he, instead of, say, Tybalt or Bingo, is the father of any children born and that both parents are in a cooperative frame of mind when the time comes to raise those children.

These pups became the fifth, sixth, seventh, and eighth members of our dog community, and were born before dawn one May morning after a difficult night. Ignoring the whelping box we had provided, Maria chose a spot in the back of my closet and stayed there right up to the time her labor began. Her courage failed her at that point, though, and as the hour of delivery drew near, she panicked, and began a desperate search for a better place. Up and down the stairs she toiled, frantic, weeping, her sides bulging, blood and amniotic fluid soiling her beautiful breeches. Misha was with his owners, but Bingo and Violet were at home, watching, and eased themselves out of her way each time she hurried by. Nothing that any of us could do or say made her feel any calmer. Without experience and facing the most critical moment of her life, she was terrified and very much alone.

Eventually she chose to get on my bed with me, and not a moment too soon. Out came a white pup — to become my beloved sled dog Suessi, a victorious hero of the winter trails who in his later years voyaged freely like his father, not in the city but in the woods, where he found and married a coyote. But all that is another story. At the time I'm speaking of, he had hardly drawn breath before he was followed by a black pup, his formidable brother Windigo. He in turn was followed by a pair of twins, a male and a female, Zooey and Moira, gray and white like Misha. When the birthing started, Maria cried for a moment, but almost immediately she put aside her fear and pain and got right to work. A competent creature, she tucked her head under her raised thigh and, with her mouth at her vulva, freed each emerging infant of its caul. Working fast, licking with her tongue, nipping with her incisors, Maria lifted the caul from each pup's nostrils, drawing the membrane back into her mouth until the pup was out to the hips, with the caul gathered like a little shirt around the umbilicus and with the cord lying between Maria's sharp carnassial teeth. Then she bit, cutting the cord and swallowing the caul even as she was nosing the pup toward her belly. In this way she was ready to swallow the afterbirth the moment it slipped out. So quickly did she manage each delivery, and so clean did she keep her body, her pups, and her nest, that by the time the fourth pup, little Moira, had been safely delivered there was no cleaning left to do. Maria then clapped her thigh against her belly and curled herself tight like a fist. And much to my surprise, she raised her eyes and stared at me, almost with hostility. *What are you looking at?* she seemed to ask.

What indeed? It seemed I could see nothing at all except the firmly clenched Maria, her head and ears high, her eyes hard, her gaze steady and direct, as if she were pointing in my direction and at the same time pointing to the door. Thighs are to dogs what arms are to humans when it comes to sheltering babies, and Maria's tight thighs hid her pups as if they had never been. *Are you okay? Would you like a drink of water?* I asked, offering her the bowl. She stared at me coldly as if I were a stranger. So I left. I came back later and tried to open her thigh so I could see the puppies. Her facial expression didn't change, but she clenched even tighter. I saw I wasn't going to see her pups unless I was prepared to brace myself and use plenty of force to unclamp her, which I didn't want to do. Instead, I offered water, milk, and food. But these were not what she wanted. People out of the room was what she wanted, so I left her again. The third time I visited her, she decided to trust me briefly, tore downstairs and outside to relieve herself, then tore back all out of breath, hopped on the bed, and settled herself with her infants, by then all warm and pink and clean, and all pushed carefully together in a pile, fast asleep. From then on, and for the rest of her long life, she was a dedicated and excellent mother, a dog madonna. Rightly was she named Maria.

The next day, Misha's owners brought him by to meet his puppies. None of us was prepared for what happened. Misha trotted into the room as usual, brisk and friendly, but at the sight of Maria he stopped dead in his tracks and his manner changed abruptly. Very slowly, he seemed to sink a little as he lowered his head, his ears, and his tail, and he stood motionless, all alone in the middle of the room, looking at Maria. She by then had been urged to use a suitable whelping box, and on the far side of the room she was lying in it, her body curled and iron fist that clenched her infants to her breasts. Her head was high, though, her ears were up straight, and her eyes were opened wide, and she stared intently over the edge of the box at Misha. Her lips were drawn back but showed only her incisors, while the stiffness of her face showed that she might gape at a moment's notice and show her eyeteeth too. But if her face was without welcome, it was also without fear. Here was a dog who was ready to fling herself at anything for the sake of her pups, but who, at least on this occasion, didn't really think she'd have to try. For a moment the two dogs simply looked at each other, Maria's expression very forthright, very sharp, alert, and Misha's very gentle, reassuring, almost cautious. Then slowly, quietly, Misha lowered his head even more, heaved his stomach, and, never taking his eyes from Maria's, he vomited.

The members of Misha's human audience all spoke up at once, offering theories to explain his seemingly strange act. Perhaps the thought of the puppies was making him nervous. Perhaps excitement or jealousy was making him sick. Yet those were not his reasons for vomiting. In fact, he was telling Maria that he would feed her and their children. He was giving her the food he happened to have with him at the moment, and the gift was a promise of more. Thus do adult wolves provision their young.

The mystery offered by Misha, therefore, was not why did he vomit but how did he know about the pups? There he was, just two years old, raised by people, and inexperienced in dog paternity. He certainly hadn't seen the puppies, deep in the box, held tight between Maria's flank and thigh. Not even God got to see Maria's puppies. So how did Misha know they were there? That question is not easily answered. Since the pups made no noise, he couldn't have heard them, and since — at least to a human being — they were odorless, he probably couldn't have smelled them either. If he had, however, how could he know what the smell meant? Unquestionably, Maria's demeanor would have told him that something was different from the time he'd seen her last, but lacking experience, how could he know what her demeanor said? He knew, though. No dog has ever shown more clearly that he knew what he was dealing with than Misha did that morning.

As a father, Misha was something like the Baffin wolves. When his pups were small, he didn't really like having them around his ankles but preferred to be higher than they were, so that if they were on the floor, he'd get up on a chair or the sofa. When his pups were about four months old, he sometimes took the eldest one voyaging. At first I was horrified to find Misha and the white pup gone (Misha had jumped the fence and the pup had squeezed under it through a freshly dug tunnel), not only because Misha's parenting skills were unproven but also because I knew of no behavioral precedent in wolves, whereby Misha could have consulted his instincts if questions arose. In my mind's eye I saw Misha getting interested in something else and forgetting his pup, who would then be far from home and lost without a guide. But that never happened. As time passed, it became clear that Misha never traveled very far when tender little Suessi was with him. And evidently he didn't travel very fast, or cross dangerous highways, or venture into the territory of the Saint Bernard. Mostly, as far as I could tell, he passed through people's back yards or kept to the borders of a large cemetery, where the traffic was slow and where dangerous dogs wouldn't rush out to surprise them. If I hadn't by chance met one of the groundskeepers at the cemetery, I might never have learned where these dogs had been, since I couldn't in conscience condone voyaging with an inexperienced puppy even if Misha had invited me to go along, which he had not.

However, I suspect that the white pup, Suessi, got his unparalleled navigational skills from traveling as a youngster with his father — skills that served him well throughout his long and interesting life, dramatically so one subzero night in New Hampshire when, ancient, quite feeble, and stricken with Alzheimer's disease, he wandered off into the woods during a blizzard. Perhaps he had been thinking of his coyote woman, who had disappeared from the area some time before. Frantic, I ran out across the fields searching and calling, and at last I saw his rickety form striding along through the whirling snow, heading not for my voice but for the house. Possibly because of his father's good teaching eighteen years earlier, any confusion his Alzheimer's may have caused him did not apply to where he was going.

SUESSI WAS the firstborn pup, and grew up to be the highest-ranking of the litter. He remained the highest-ranking male in our group after Misha. Second to him was the next pup born, the black male, Windigo, and third was the male twin, Zooey. Bingo didn't count as far as the huskies were concerned, except that the pups, while young, respected him. Suessi and Windigo were almost identical in height and weight, and the social difference between them was almost imperceptible. They spent their lives together, always in perfect friendship. They never fought each other, and only once that I know of joined together to fight anyone else. Their adversary was a friend's young brown-and-white husky, whom I had agreed to house temporarily. To my surprise, the young husky combined social ignorance with an unrealistic idea of his own power, and actually tried to dominate my older dogs. For a long time they ignored him. If dogs are thinking of fighting, they usually do so very shortly after meeting or not at all, and when nothing happened, I assumed that all was well and left the group alone.

Evidently Suessi and Windigo felt no need to prove themselves to the stranger, or to teach him a lesson, or to force him to acknowledge their high status. However, that didn't mean they were prepared to tolerate his posturing forever. One day, to my astonishment, they decided simply to execute the young brown-and-white dog, and with two of their nephews beside them were closing in to do just that when I intervened. I burst through the ring of dogs and threw myself over the youngster, who for all his former arrogance understood exactly what I was trying to do for him and, aware at last of his misjudgment, made no objection to my pinning him, but instead took part in his own salvation by becoming submissive and quiet despite his wounds. My own dogs saw me merely as an obstacle and cast about for a way around me to their victim. From my position on the ground, with their intense faces almost touching mine, I could look straight into their eyes, and I saw there no anger, no fear, no threat, no show of aggression, just clarity and over-whelming determination. Such is the psychological power of high status, at least in dogs.

Virtually all dogfights are caused by disagree-ments over status, which are questions of rank, re-ally, and interestingly enough even cause dogs to bite children. Many dogs willingly and gracefully submit to human adults, but they'll be darned if they'll do the same for human children, who as any-one can see have not yet earned high status. At that, many such bites are not really bites at all, but merely whacks with the teeth, disciplinary acts that dogs use on their own children, something that, as far as I can tell, dogs do only when in one way or another their children are insufficiently submissive, or, in other words, presume upon the older dog's higher status. When a dog wants to discipline her puppies, she bares her front teeth to the gums and cracks the puppy hard with the side of a long canine, often accompanying the blow with a short but frightening roar. This all happens very fast and of course looks like a terrible bite to horrified human observers, es-pecially if the dog thus disciplines a human child, but it isn't a bite, and the technique explains why many dogs who appear to bite children don't actually break the skin.

Unlike the brown-and-white husky, most dogs learn to acknowledge the high status of their betters very early in puppyhood. This once saved the life of a little Yorkshire terrier who, dressed in a plaid jacket and boots and wearing a ribbon in his hair, was jiggling along on a leash past my house. I was just setting out on a trip, and my dogs were on the sidewalk, ready to get in the car, when to my horror they shot off after the little creature. Worse yet, instead of pausing at a distance from the Yorkie, as dogs do when meeting another dog, they rushed straight to him, as dogs do when catching a rabbit or cat. I screamed, the Yorkie's owner screamed, but most important, the Yorkie himself screamed and rolled on his back. This stopped my dogs in their tracks. Horrified and suddenly very still, they stared down at the rigid little creature at their feet, who, his tail tight between his legs, was looking up at them while passing urine. What had happened? Alas, the Yorkie's owner had soaked him in cologne. That and his clothes had disguised him so successfully that my dogs mistook him for some other species. Probably they didn't bother to wonder what he was; the important thing to them was what he was not — a dog like themselves, subject to all rights and privileges thereto. His own quick thinking, not me or his terrified owner, saved his life. The acts of rolling on his back, tucking his tail and passing urine like a puppy, and even his scream unmasked him and, like dog passwords of species and low status, alerted his would-be hunters just in time.

As long as dogs of low status know and keep their place, they need not fear attack from high-ranking dogs. In addition, a respectful show of low rank can assure membership in a group to a dog who would be excluded if he seemed to rival the group's high-ranking members. Dogs like their societies to be well ordered, and to this end rank themselves as if on the rungs of a ladder, the males at one side, the females at the other. In some dog societies the hierarchy system is so willingly embraced that friction is rarely observed. And that is the point, really. Knowing who is who eliminates strife and fighting.

PERFECT SOCIAL equilibrium can be hard to attain. This became clear to us and our dogs the year after Maria's pups were born, when our group suffered some profound changes. That spring, Misha's owners gave him away. We of course wanted to keep him, but some of our neighbors, with the law on their side, were so bitterly opposed to him that we could not. Instead, his owners found a home for him in another state, a house in the country with people who were good to dogs, so we believe he was happy, except that he would have missed his family. His family pined for him. Both he and Maria knew that something was terribly wrong when his owners came for him the last time, so that Maria struggled to follow him out the door. When she was prevented, she rushed to the windowseat and, with her back to the room, watched Misha being forced into the car. She stayed in the window for weeks thereafter, sitting backward on the seat with her face to the window and her tail to the room, watching and waiting for Misha. At last she must have realized he wasn't going to come. Something happened to her at that point. She lost her radiance and became depressed. She moved more slowly, was less responsive, and got angry rather easily at things that before she would have overlooked. She also showed less interest in her children, although they were almost grown by then.

Her unhappiness broke my heart. I took to giving her a scoop of ice cream late every afternoon, at about the time Misha would have visited. She would brighten briefly and eat the ice cream — she liked ice cream — so I suppose it helped her for the little time the taste was on her tongue. But even for a dog, food as a panacea doesn't really work. Maria never recovered from her loss, and although she never forfeited her place as alpha female, she showed no interest in forming a permanent bond with another male, even though, over the years, several eligible males joined our household.

That spring Maria's daughter, Moira, left with her owner, a student who had lived in our house, and Moira's twin brother, Zooey, left to live with my husband's brother's family. That fall an infant female dingo, Viva, and a mature female husky, Koki, entered the picture. Viva was so small I put her in my shirt to keep her warm, fed her with a baby bottle, and helped her to eliminate by stroking her inguinal region with a cotton ball, as her mother would have done with her tongue.

The husky, Koki, was an Indian dog, born in a Native American village in Alaska. She was a slave, born on the snow to live at the end of a chain. Yet she was an athlete, a sled dog, and one of the most intelligent creatures I ever knew. I wanted her to be the leader of a dog team, a task she performed to perfection once she had gotten over her fears. Evidently dog life was less than roseate in the far northern villages: the sound of something whizzing through the air — a rope, perhaps, or a stick — would reduce Koki to jelly, so that she would sink to the ground with her hair on end, her teeth chattering and her eyes blazing with fear. So would the sound of alcohol in a man's voice. He didn't have to be drunk to terrify her; just the hint in the voice would be enough. She never got over these terrors, but she did learn that on our dog team nobody would hurt her, even if something went wrong while she was leading and therefore supposedly responsible. And besides, she was grateful to me. So she and I enjoyed the winter trails for years thereafter. Meanwhile, she had to integrate herself with the other dogs.

At first she was alternately hostile to them and fearful of them, which showed a lot, I thought, about her early experiences as a sled dog. Maria didn't like Koki any more than Koki liked Maria, and they flew at each other every chance they got. Their bodies and my hands and arms got badly torn by the fights that followed. Needless to say, I tried to keep the two females separated, and most of the time I succeeded. While Koki stayed around my office and the front yard, Maria stayed around the kitchen and back yard with the other dogs. Koki had me, but Maria had the pack. When we went dogsledding, Maria stayed home or in the car (she had a bad foot) while Koki led the others. So, although Koki eventually befriended the other dogs and got to be the alpha female during working hours, Maria was the true, recognized alpha dog, unquestionably Dog One over all the males and the females, including Koki, and everybody knew it.

Not surprisingly, Maria's ascendancy over Koki did not mean that she accepted Koki into the group, but rather that she had the authority to drive Koki away, and thus the separation of the two females continued to be essential. The arrangement kept both dogs reasonably content until early spring, when they went into heat.

Who knows what brings dogs into heat. Long nights and short days? Short days getting longer? Other dogs in heat? Undetected pheromones? Something else? Whatever it is, although dogs have no breeding season any more than we do, dogs in groups, like people in groups, tend to ovulate together. Among my dogs, the high-ranking females tended to start the process, and that year young Viva, the dingo, was also affected by the mystery and came into heat too. Little Bingo, the pug, showed these ladies that he was willing to be their husband, but not one of them seemed to take him seriously.

Who gets to reproduce in a group of wild canids? Only the dominant pair, of course, since to raise just one litter takes the strenuous effort of everyone in the pack. But if one of the dominant pair is missing, what then? If the female is missing, the male might mate with one of his daughters. Apparently father-daughter incest doesn't seem too reprehensible to members of the dog family. But mother-son incest seems to be a different story. For reasons known to dogs but not to us, many dog mothers won't mate with their sons. Certainly Maria wouldn't. Oddly enough, though, the taboo that Maria felt so strongly was not shared by her sons, who had no reticence about approaching her. Both kept badgering her, and at last became very insistent. Suessi even caught her by the tail and dragged her to him. She wouldn't have them, though, and she wouldn't turn her back to them lest they surprise her. Instead, when they came too near she would face them, sit down, and show them her teeth.

In contrast, Koki and Viva could have chosen any of the males. Strangely enough, however, neither female showed any sign of wanting to mate with anyone. As far as I could see, they didn't mark or display or invite. To human eyes there was no obvious reason for this. Yet I expect that in a subtle way, Maria was coercing them. In the wild, alpha female wolves are often able to keep their subordinates from getting pregnant by sheer force of personality: the alphas disapprove of the subordinates receiving males, and the subordinates know it. Alpha female wolves communicate their feelings by staring at subordinate females when the males come around, and usually the stare is enough to make the subordinates sit down. This, it seemed, was what Maria was doing to Koki and Viva, who for as long as the heat lasted seemed very subdued. But I wanted Koki bred, because I knew her children would be very good sled dogs, and after removing her to a place where Maria wouldn't know what she was doing, I put her together with Suessi.

Possibly males are also mildly coerced by social expectations. Suessi was almost equally unenthusiastic. But I kept the dogs together until they joined. All went well. During the act they were quite touchingly tender with each other, although they got little joy from the exercise as a whole, and when it was over they parted without further ado. Surely Maria realized what had happened — afterward she went up to Suessi and very deliberately smelled his penis, to which the odors of Koki and of the mating would still have clung.

A few days later Maria's third son, Zooey, came back to live with us because my husband's brother's family couldn't adapt to his roaming. Zooey had hardly stepped through the doorway when Maria ran straight to him, spun herself around, held aside her tail, and would have received him then and there if we hadn't stopped them. Her willingness opened a mystery: why would she have him but not his brothers? She knew, we didn't. Possibly she didn't recognize Zooey. He had been a youngster when he left, almost a year earlier, and he was a full-grown adult when he returned. At that, he had the odors of another household on him. No wonder if she didn't remember who he was. However, after an absence of more than two years, one of Koki's daughters returned for a visit, and everyone present, our family as well as the daughter's owners, believed that Koki and her daughter recognized each other.

But whether Maria recognized Zooey or not really didn't matter. After all, the only thing Maria wanted from Zooey was to be inseminated. Otherwise, then and later, she made no effort to be with him, or to play or travel with him as she had done with Misha. He had been third from the top of the male hierarchy when he left us, and he immediately and willingly took the same place when he returned, possibly because his former status clung to him, or possibly because places one and two were taken by established dogs more forceful than he. And possibly Maria didn't want him as a permanent consort because of his relatively low rank. Whether or not she saw him as a stranger, she didn't see him as a suitable mate.

Love between dogs is very moving, but equally moving, in my view, is a businesslike sexual encounter, wherein a female who cares little or nothing for the male seeks only to get herself bred. One functional mating I happened to witness seemed particularly impersonal, and surely something like it was what Maria had in mind. The episode took place on a sidewalk in San Jose, Costa Rica, where a little female stood for a high-ranking male. Four other males waited for a turn while one male (Dog Two in the assembled hierarchy) guarded the joined pair, snapping mildly at human passersby who came too near. After coming apart, in contrast to Misha and Maria, who had rejoiced together, the Costa Rican dogs didn't even exchange a glance but, with their backs to each other, sat right down on opposite sides of the pavement and spent the next few minutes cleaning their genitals. Finished, the female stood up, but the action brought a fresh discharge of semen, so she sat down and cleaned herself again. When she was through, the high-ranking dog had gone. She walked away, trailed by the other males in order of rank, each paying more attention to the others' whereabouts than any of them paid to her. Like people waiting in line for concert tickets, expecting to enjoy the show without interacting with the performer, the males seemed mainly concerned that no one jump the line. Maria's mating would have been dispassionate like that.

I would have liked to conclude the observation, if

only to see how the female acted with the other males, but I couldn't. Unfortunately, it was evening, and the sidewalk chosen by the dogs was just outside a noisy bar in an otherwise deserted, low-rent section of the city. I was with the science writer Sy Montgomery, and it struck us that the patrons of the bar might misinterpret the motive of two unaccompanied North American women on an empty street at night, watching dogs copulate. The possibility was daunting, so we left.

WHEN AT LAST little Viva, the dingo, came into heat, she knew her place, and showed us all that she had no thought of receiving a male, certainly not while Maria continued to stare disapprovingly. Who, after all, was Viva to give birth? If the group had been wild and had been trying to maintain a den, Viva would not have been the mother; Viva would have been one of the hunting helpers and babysitters, if indeed her presence had been tolerated at all. I had been letting her into our yard alone to relieve herself, which she did very circumspectly, not marking at all and coming inside right afterward as requested. One day, however, as I was watching her out the window, I saw a springer spaniel flying through the air. Over the fence he soared, and crashed down beside Viva in a spray of gravel and grass. His name, I later learned, was Misty, but at the time he was a total stranger. His sudden appearance terrified Viva, who, being wild, was intolerant of surprises, and very shy as well. She ran for the kitchen door and so did I, bursting out just as the spaniel jumped on top of her. Screaming like a dog who has been hit by a car, she rolled onto her back with her tail clamped up tight between her legs to cover her vulva, an attitude of unqualified resistance and at the same time of terrified sub-ordination. But the spaniel bravely bestrode her. Although Viva fought him, twisting, screaming, kicking, and biting, and although I shouted and waved my arms as I galloped toward them, in the time it took me to cross the yard the springer had penetrated her and had locked. So there was nothing to do but wait, me fuming, the terrified dingo strug-gling to get up and crying bitterly, and the spaniel quite apologetic, standing astride her but looking up at me with some anxiety to learn if he was in danger. He wasn't, of course — dog actions can't be judged by human values — and when the two came apart I opened the gate and let him go in peace. After all, he had taught us something: that dogs can rape.

Thus ended the heat. Koki was pregnant by Suessi, Viva was pregnant by the spaniel (we tried mismating shots, to no avail), and Maria, who as alpha female should by dog rules have been the only dog pregnant, was not pregnant at all. Two months passed. Koki was ready to give birth. Since these pups were my idea, not Koki's or anybody else's, I arranged a whelping box in my office where she could deliver unobserved and unmolested — this was a human event, not a dog event, as I saw it. Koki understood. She gave birth quite easily and well to five nice puppies, but her nest, when she had finished, wasn't as clean as Maria's had been, and she didn't hold her pups as closely. Furthermore, although she smiled when people came to see her and showed her pups quite readily, she sometimes seemed uneasy, spent less time in her box than Maria had spent, and often felt irritated by the pups. Late one night she hit her little firstborn male very hard with the side of her bared eyetooth, and his crying brought everyone, dog and human alike, to the door of the room. Although the pup was out on the floor, still crying, Koki lay back in her box as if nothing were happening.

All this does not mean she was not a good mother.

She was a fine mother, who protected her children and for the most part treated them well. She just wasn't like Maria. But after all, motherhood meant different things to these two dogs because of their extremely different experiences. Maria had given birth on my bed in complete safety. She had had a husband who loved her plus the support and assistance of everyone around her — not only Misha and the human beings but also the two pugs, who had functioned in that context as secondary or assistant dogs. Koki's first experience in birthing, by contrast, had been in a far northern dog yard at the end of a chain. Judging from her perceived need to fight for survival the moment she entered our door, Koki's relationship with her former teammates hadn't been friendly. Not for her the sense of security that Maria enjoyed. And for her second litter, how did Koki envision the pups' future? Two pups of Maria's first litter were still with her as adults two years later. Who knows what had happened to Koki's first pups or how young they had been when taken from her. Maria's first experience with birthing had made her intense and passionate. Koki's first experience had made her sad and afraid.

Yet perhaps Koki's uneasiness had to do with the future as well as the past. Surely Koki knew that Viva was pregnant, and felt that she would need to take steps to save her own children. Poor little Viva certainly understood that something was wrong; she cried a lot and clung to me as the time of her delivery drew near. At eight months old, she herself was only a child, and she was frightened. My husband happened to be away just then, so Viva slept beside me on the bed. She stayed under my feet as I sat at my desk, and crept along between me and the wall as I moved about the house. I had an outside job in those days and couldn't take her with me, but I took time off on her due date. She delivered on my bed in the dead of night, curled up tight against me, and although she seemed to be in quite a bit of pain she managed everything rather slowly but fairly well. In two hours she delivered five tender little pups, three males and two females, all the same size, all with the same short, silky hair, and all grayish brown, the color of the earth, the birth color of all wild puppies.

Of the three mothers, Viva seemed by far the least adept. She was young, it was true, but Maria, the canine Earth Mother, had only been a few months older than Viva when she had so successfully delivered her first litter. But Maria had wanted puppies, and Viva, it seemed, did not. This is not to say she didn't love them. She never seemed annoyed or troubled by them, and she didn't reject them. On the contrary, she approached them very tenderly, if tentatively. As if they were not hers but she wished they were, they seemed to make her sad. She nursed them often enough, but otherwise spent very little time holding them close. Rather, she left them piled together for warmth in a nest I had made for her right beside my bed, while she sat bolt upright, tense and stiff, in the middle of the room, obviously distressed and sometimes trembling, as if she were afraid to be with her pups and at the same time afraid to leave them.

After two or three days I returned to work, leaving Viva with her pups in my bedroom, Koki with her pups in the kitchen, and the other dogs outside, where they wouldn't bother the new mothers, all under the supervision of other human members of our household, including a housekeeper. But when I came home in the afternoon I could feel that something terrible had happened. The house was absolutely silent. My children were out, as was their custom at that time of day; my husband was away, and the housekeeper was resting. All that was as it should be. So the trouble was not with the human beings. But usually when we came home the dogs would greet us. That day nobody appeared, and the deep silence went on. I went partway up the stairs. There sat Viva, shrinking and trembling, outside my bedroom door. In silence, she looked at me. I listened, and heard toenails scratching as someone took uneven, nervous steps on the bedroom floor. A dog who had been standing still was moving. I went up the stairs past Viva and into the bedroom. Viva's nest was empty, and Koki, looking extremely distressed, was walking hesitantly toward me with a pup in her mouth. I asked her to give it to me, and bending her head slightly she placed it very simply on the floor. Then she turned and left the room. I heard her toenails on the stairs. She was slowly going down to her own puppies.

The puppy, a female, was unhurt. I put her back in the nest and searched the house and found the rest of Viva's puppies lying dead in various places where Koki had carried them and killed them. Two were cool and one was starting to stiffen. Two were still limp, and one of these was quite warm. Koki had killed them over a long period of time, perhaps more than an hour. And she had killed them by shaking them, because no blood showed. Outside, the other dogs had clustered together and were looking in at us through a glass door. I believe they understood what had happened and must have seen at least one killing — one corpse lay within sight of the door. I would have expected a killing to excite the dogs profoundly, but instead they seemed extremely subdued. Brave little Bingo was standing very still with his feet on the doorstep, looking at me with bulging eyes and flattened ears. Even his tail was uncurled dismally.

So there we stood, all of us looking at one another through the glass while I tried to understand what the dogs already knew: that from a dog point of view, the killings had been unavoidable. And so they were. If the dogs saw themselves as a group, and if a group can raise only one litter, there cannot be two litters. Koki was a high-status dog and Viva was a low-status dog. Koki's pups had the right to live and Viva's pups didn't. Koki did what she had to do, and the other dogs knew it. Even Viva knew it, which explained her detachment from the pups. She could have fought Koki; at other times and in other situations she had even defeated Koki. But that day she had stood quietly aside, as if even she believed that her pups had no right to be born.

Perhaps more touching, more interesting, than Viva's feelings were Koki's feelings. Her nervousness and repressed agitation spoke of her unwillingness to kill puppies — after all, dogs are like us in that they instinctively recognize infancy, a recognition that releases caregiving behavior in dogs just as it does in human beings. Hence, to take a child and kill it, not in anger or in desperation but out of conviction that one is doing the right thing, is almost impossible, either for a dog or for a human being. Yet Koki had managed just that. Her coat looked disheveled and rough when I first caught sight of her holding the pup, I believe because adrenaline had put her hair on end. And her walk was almost prancing, as if she were jumping out of her skin. When I asked for the pup she gave it almost gladly, as if she didn't want to hurt it. She laid it down instead of merely opening her mouth and dropping it. I felt she was relieved that I had come in to assume responsibility for the situation.

When I looked at the still bodies of poor Viva's pups, I couldn't help but think of human hunter-gatherers, the Ju/wa Bushmen of the Kalahari Desert of southern Africa, with whom I had lived as a young woman. In those days the Ju/wasi fed and clothed themselves entirely from the savannah; their lives were led very far from so-called civilization, with almost no contact with any people but their own. Sometimes, on rare occasions, a Ju/wa mother would give birth to an infant who couldn't be supported, an infant who would compete with an older sibling still too young to leave the breast. Then the mother would have to force herself to commit infanticide. It was a terrible thing, unquestionably, but the alternative was worse — malnutrition and death not only for the infant but also for the toddler.

Rather than lose both children, the mother killed the newborn at birth, almost as Koki had done. Then I saw how much a pack is one thing, with each member as a part of it. Like parts of a body, they function together on behalf of the whole. Life is only for the brave, or so it is for those who live in the old way, by the old rules.

THE PUP who survived was named Fatima by
our daughter, for a favorite teacher. Viva was
very reluctant to take care of this pup, or even to get
into the nest with her. Maria, however, had no such
fears. Maria marched up to the nest, grabbed the
pup, whisked her away to my daughter's room,
jumped up on the bed, tucked little Fatima into her
groin, and clamped shut the fist of her body. There
they remained. My daughter and I got out the artificial bitch's milk, and the raising of Fatima began.
There was no question now of any danger to Fa-

tima; always alert, Maria readily displayed the length of her teeth to any dog unwise enough to venture into the room, and would almost have relished an encounter with Koki. But Koki stayed with her own pups, continued her rather flaccid mothering, and kept far away. The next day I happened to see one bare nipple in a tiny halo of damp fur stuck to Maria's belly. Little Fatima had been suckling. On the third day I was shocked to see two bare, damp nipples and a drop of milk! As if miraculously, Maria was lactating.

Is adoption natural for dogs? Strangely enough, it seems to be, just as it is natural for people. Both species are stirred to do it by inner forces that neither species really understands. Unfortunately, when a dog or a person lactates without pregnancy, she rarely, if ever, produces enough milk to raise a foundling, but that in no way suppresses our powerful desire to embrace someone very young. Even the species of the foundling doesn't much matter. Once my daughter and I found a dead opossum by the side of a country road and noticed something moving on her belly. It turned out to be her pouch stuffed full of fetuses, four of whom were living. We took them. They were no bigger than beetle grubs, whom they resembled; they had no eyes or ears and only buds for fingers. Nevertheless, we took them home, dug out the artificial bitch's milk, and began to feed them.

Was our behavior atavistic? Perhaps so, but perhaps we merely felt a sense of obligation. At that stage of their development, the naked little possums were very far from what our species finds appealing. Some people were almost frightened by the sight of one of them feeding, since they were small enough to wrap their arms and legs around the eyedropper and cling head down, licking milk from the tip. The spectacle was disgusting, people said, like a thick worm stuck to the eyedropper, or like a baby rat. And so it was, to our kind. Yet when I saw how Koki watched the young opossums, I put one down on the floor. I had seen that she wasn't going to harm it. On the floor the fetal possum tumbled very slowly over and over, grasping at itself in the absence of anything else to hold on to. Immediately Koki crouched over it, extended her chin stiffly above it, and looked up at me with hard, emotional eyes, the posture of a dog above an object that has enormous significance — a fresh beef condyle, perhaps, or a newborn pup. Koki was very firm about protecting the young possum, and although it was too small for her to lift with her mouth, she would have nosed it into the warmth of her body had I not picked it up to return it to its nest.

What about the possum had Koki liked? Probably its groping, tumbling motion, its blunt face, its lack of eyes, and its nudity, all characteristics shared by neonatal dog pups, who perhaps are not nude but who seem nude because their fur is fine and short.

In just a few weeks, the possums outgrew their fetal appearance. About the size of baby chicks, they had bright eyes, delicate pink Mickey Mouse ears, short tails, and little coats of fur that stood on end like thistledown. Now, as they scampered back and forth in their glass terrarium, people found them adorable, talked baby talk to them, and wanted to cuddle them. Not Koki, though. Koki watched them through the glass with gleaming eyes. She wanted to catch them. To her, they no longer seemed like infants in need of mothering, but like prey.

About a year after the infanticide, Koki, like Maria, had an opportunity to adopt pups when the dingo, Viva, had a second litter, by a sled dog who belonged to a friend in New Hampshire. Viva still felt too low in status to keep for herself something as valuable to her as her own pups, and as the hour of her delivery drew near, she suffered. Again she clung to me. I tried to reassure her, but after her last experience she understandably didn't believe me. By day as I worked at my desk she sat stiffly beside me, overcome with dread, her back straight, her head bowed, her tail tense, her legs as close together as her swollen belly would allow, as if she were poised to run and until then would try to occupy as little space as possible. By night she lay on my bed, pressed against me. Her feelings drained her energy. When her labor began late one night, she was too tired or too depressed to bear down strongly, and between contractions she seemed exhausted. At last she rolled onto her back, and with her legs spread, her nipples erect, and her belly jumping from the activity inside, she fell into a fitful sleep and dreamed of her own infancy.

How did I know the subject of a dingo's dream? I knew by the shape of Viva's mouth. A puppy when nursing curls its tongue into a U and shapes its cheeks forward — a dramatic and unmistakable configuration of the mouth seen at no other time. Viva did this. Was she remembering a time when her own cares were few? Possibly, except that her first weeks of life had been spent on frozen manure inside an ice cold, pitch-dark barn belonging to the animal dealer from whom I rescued her. I had had to leave her starving mother and siblings behind, even though I had seen that her mother was in such dire physical condition that she couldn't give much care to her pups. Was Viva returning to this in her dream? Or did she feel her own four pups about to be born, and was she imagining herself in their place? In her sleep, she cried and sucked, cried and sucked, and when at last she woke up she was delivering.

All went well. Again she gave birth to pups with earth-colored fur — wild coloring. And again she felt the social criticism of the other dogs, even through the walls of the securely closed room in which I kept her. She wouldn't stay in the nest with her pups, and one day, when Koki looked in through the briefly opened door, Viva moved aside as if inviting her to enter. So Koki came in. But this time, because Koki had no litter of her own, she didn't want to kill Viva's puppies but to protect and cuddle them, and that is what she did. Like Maria, she also produced milk.

Her milk and loving care, plus more artificial bitch's milk, helped the pups grow strong and healthy. In time they became the most beautiful dogs that I, for one, had ever seen. Tall and well proportioned, they had their dingo mother's red-gold hair and their husky father's blue eyes, and many people wanted to adopt one. Unfortunately, the youngest, a female, died in early adolescence from a herniated esophagus, a birth defect, and we gave the middle two away, but Koki kept the eldest, a female named Inookshook, who proved to be as loyal to Koki as Fatima was to Maria. Born of the same mother, Fatima and Inookshook should have resembled each other in personality, but in fact these dingo sisters took after their foster mothers, so that Fatima, like Maria, was intense and active, while Inookshook, like Koki, was quiet and deep.

In a sense, Inookshook was the third generation in our group, or was to the others what a pup of the Baffin Island wolves was to the pack: a youngster with parents and full-grown siblings, who in Inookshook's case perhaps were not biologically related but certainly were socially and emotionally influential. In consequence, Inookshook had not only stunning beauty but also elegant manners. We made no attempt to teach her anything, not even housebreaking. Quietly, her elders taught her that and also everything else she ever needed to know, and the result was perfection.

Once we took her to a forest where a great many sled dog teams were tethered prior to a race in which our son participated (and at which, thanks to Suessi and Windigo, he won a gigantic iridescent trophy decorated with dogs and eagles and topped with a

Winged Victory). Inookshook was to join one of the teams temporarily but had never met the dogs. When she saw through the trees where we were leading her, she seemed a little apprehensive, and rightly so, since the twenty or so strange dogs, all tied to a long chain, were rising to their feet, snarling and bristling at her. She hesitated for a moment, as if taking note of the problem. And then, instead of turning tail to retreat or fighting the leash that held her, she advanced smoothly and slowly. Perhaps like her stepgrandfather, Misha (whom she never knew), she wanted to appear serene to the ferocious strangers, and not to let them see that she was being forced or was in any way discomfited. She didn't fold her ears or tuck her tail, but like a princess walked gracefully forward as if she were sure of her welcome and wanted to approach. Not until she was less than thirty feet away did she bow her head politely, smiling and softly friendly, as if anticipating only good, and then, incredible as it sounds, she actually dropped a curtsy to the snarling strangers, bending her hind legs outward at the knees and — thighs akimbo — lowering the rear of her body. A dog at this point passes a little urine, a token of youth that says to her audience, *You are powerful adults and I know it — in your presence I am merely a pup.* So said Inookshook, and the effect on the twenty fierce adults was almost magical. At once they all lowered their hair, relaxed their lips, averted their eyes, and let her come among them as if they had known her forever.

Of course, we would never part with such a dog — anyway, she was only away on a short-term loan — and we soon brought her back to the heart of her group, where she lived on for the rest of her life as Koki's daughter and assistant. To be sure, she was low in the hierarchy owing to parentage and generation, but she was so graceful about it, so accepting of her station, that the other dogs never reminded her of it, so that more often than not she seemed like a high-ranking dog.

WHAT WAS IT like, living in the city in a house with six or eight dogs? There was nothing to it, really. Dingoes and certain sled dogs are alike in a way, so delicate of manner, so clean and quiet, that one hardly knows they are around. Ours seemed like cats in that domestication meant little to them, and they seemed like coyotes or jackals in that they were very strong but also very light in weight, and therefore moved silently. When moving about, the pugs made much more noise than the larger dogs, because the pugs walked more clumsily.

Also, only the pugs took much interest in the human life around them, so only the pugs barked. Of course, most animals bark a little — which is to say that if surprised and puzzled simultaneously, most animals, including human beings, make a short, sharp call; the call is "Huh?" in our species. Highly domesticated dogs make an art of their puzzlement and bark insistently, alerting others to unexplained events. But not the huskies, who didn't bark at human-generated sounds or happenings any more than they barked at birds in the sky, and surely for the same reason: the doings of the birds and the people lacked significance for them.

In contrast, the dogs took an unlimited interest in each other. When a dog returned after a brief absence, the others would quietly surround him and investigate him for scent — the scents of his own body, which would show his state of mind and probably a great deal more as well, and the scents of the place he had been, which he carried on his fur. They'd smell his lips and his mantle, his penis, his legs and his feet. Seldom, if ever, would they investigate his anus or anal glands, evidently because the information therefrom has to do with a dog's persona but not with his travels. The dogs would investigate me, too, particularly if I had been away a long time. They paid special attention to my legs from the knees down, as if I had been wading through odors.

Gentle and graceful as they were, they made me think of wolves. They traveled like wolves. We often think of wolves traveling in large groups, sweeping through the forests in packs. And so they do, especially in winter when the whole group is on the move, with no plans to go back to the same place. Otherwise, they tend to travel singly or in pairs. So did the dogs, since they always returned to our house when their traveling was over. Interestingly, they traveled as a pack when they were with me and our destination was obscure. I used to cross the city with them, keeping Maria beside me with a leash while the others heeled to her or to me, so that we traveled in a cohesive, orderly group, like a swarm. Needless to say, I never trained them to do this, or anything else for that matter. I meant to see what they wanted, not a reflection of what they thought I wanted.

Mostly, they wanted to live like wolves. Like wolves they dug shallow, dog-shaped depressions in the dirt, where they slept through the heat of the day, and in winter, although I welcomed them in the house and always brought them in at night, they also dug beds in the snow. After a snowfall I would often call to them in an apparently empty yard, only to see them erupt from the snowdrifts where they had buried themselves. The huskies had a particular affection for winter, especially after they became sled dogs. Their happiness and excitement increased as the days grew shorter and the nights colder, and climaxed at the first snow. They made no sound when the snow began, but one could see from their bearing that they were tense with excitement — out they would hurry, all together, to circle the yard in delight and to leap into the air to catch the falling snow.

Once I had a chance to compare them to wolves, not merely to the hard-working wolves of Baffin but to tame, household wolves whose lives resembled the lives of most dogs almost exactly. Named Jethro and Clem, these wolves represented their species at schools and other educational institutions, and were used to picket department stores that sold wolf fur. In our neighborhood, their visit caused a great stir. Our male dogs faded into the background at the sight of them, but the females came forward boldly to play. Nervous, the neighbors called the police, who, since the wolves were not illegal and could not be expelled, then maintained a constant presence in our street. But the two wolves knew nothing of the consternation they were causing. They sat together under an ornamental maple in perfect fellowship and contentment, idly watching the slowly moving patrol car as it cruised by our house, or glancing up from time to time at my dogs, who were imprisoned in an upstairs room but of course kept looking out the window.

In their attitudes, the two wolves were in every way like my dogs. Like most of my dogs, they were not related. They weren't even the same race, since one was a buffalo wolf and the other a tundra wolf. Like my dogs, they were merely good friends. Only one thing was remarkably different, at least as I saw it, which was that sometimes, perhaps to pass the time, the wolves would sing. Their voices were clear and extremely beautiful, and their songs were, quite literally, complex duets as precise as canons, with, evidently, nothing accidental or haphazard about them. The effect on human beings was electric, hair-raising. Singing seemed to give joy to the two wolves, since they rejoiced together afterward.

Usually they sang at certain times of day. For example, they sang for a long time almost every afternoon at about four o'clock, at least while they were at our house. And they sang briefly every morning. They spent their nights in a van but always knew which way was east, and incredible as it seems, when the sky grew pale they would crowd together at the van's little window with their eyes on the eastern sky. They would wait for the sun and begin to sing the moment the red rim showed over the horizon. According to their owner they had done this every day, day after day, all their adult lives together. But before they sang, they had to actually see the first red bit of the sun. Why? No person knows why. Nevertheless, their sapience was chilling.

In contrast, my dogs rarely sang. When they first heard the wolves, they fell absolutely silent and listened intently, but they didn't reply or join the song. At the time, this seemed strange. And then, when I thought about it, I realized that I'd never heard my dogs sing or howl beyond an occasional choral response to a fire engine. Wolves sing all the time, as do other packs of huskies. Noisy howling is a problem wherever large groups of dogs are quartered. In some areas, either city or country, a person can usually start most of the surrounding dogs howling, and by howling in forests scientists are sometimes able to locate wolves, who howl replies. But not my dogs. No one has ever been able to make my dogs howl. Nor would they howl on their own, either singly or together, and with two exceptions they never did, and I don't know why.

WHAT WERE the two exceptions? At the age of twelve, the pug Bingo developed urinary stones that required major surgery. Evidently his little wife, Violet, wasn't as mindless as she seemed; on the day her beloved was scheduled for surgery she realized that things weren't right, and stricken with fear, she tried vigorously to follow him as I carried him to the car. I pushed her back with my foot and shut the door. When I returned home hours later I had forgotten her, and not until she failed to show up for supper did I make a search. She had been hiding under the hall table, where she could see everything that came in the door. I called her, but she didn't come. At bedtime she wouldn't come to bed but spent the night alone in the dark hall by the door, waiting for Bingo. Soon after we put out the lights we heard a faint, strange, strangled call: little Violet was howling.

It was the first and only time I ever heard her do that. Wolves howl for assembly, and I believe Violet did too. Very simply, she was calling to Bingo. A few days later he came home. Violet's joy seemed boundless. Eyes popping, she leaped all over him, yelping and struggling for breath. Bingo took her reception calmly, being more interested in busily inspecting the house, as was his habit, to learn what had happened while he was gone.

Soon afterward he died of heart failure, while undergoing a second operation. Violet, who assumed her place under the hall table when Bingo was taken away for the second time, never again left it, except for brief visits to the yard to relieve herself and to the kitchen to eat or drink. Otherwise she crouched under the table, her eyes on the door, alert to sounds outside it. I expected her to lose her appetite from pining, but, already rotund, she continued to eat greedily, showing none of the wasting signs of sorrow. Instead, she became more nervous, more scattered, more dithering. If called to eat or to go out, she would leap to her feet and make little aimless rushes in confusion. Although I feel sure that she had never been struck by anyone in her life, she became afraid of us. If one of us tried to touch her, she jerked herself away in panic from the approaching hand. A year passed, during which she trembled with confusion under the hall table, and then she died, also of heart failure.

Then the rest of us moved to Virginia. There, because of a number of nearby horse farms, we redoubled our efforts to keep the dogs from roaming. Maria and her three sons were a bit too wolfish to be allowed to run loose around large ungulates, especially since Suessi, the highest-ranking male and firstborn brother, had once leaped at the throat of a horse, only to be kicked in the head and knocked unconscious. To restrain these dogs, we built a pen big enough for them not to feel seriously confined and not to make the usual efforts to dig their way to freedom. On the contrary, because the four leading dogs of our dog family had to stay in the pen, the other four dogs — Koki, Viva, Fatima, and Inookshook, who could always go free because they didn't chase horses — preferred to be in the pen with their seniors in the hierarchy.

One day I discovered the third-ranking, last-born husky brother, Zooey, sitting by himself in the middle of the pen, paying no attention to the life around him. He was sick, I soon learned, and I took him into my office, where he crept into the kneespace under my desk. There he stayed for the next few weeks, while the veterinarians tried unsuccessfully to find out what was the matter with him. He died at the vet's, where I had taken him yet again in a final attempt to save him. An autopsy revealed that the problem had been with his kidneys.

My view of death is quite pragmatic; as I see it, when the spirit and the life are gone, not much good comes from concerning oneself about the body. I left Zooey for the vet to bury, and I went home. It was a hazy, warm evening in the fall, I remember, and I was thinking of the next world with a new gray face in it when I noticed that all the other dogs were sitting more or less together and quietly watching me, some inside and some outside the fence. So I went to them and let them smell me.

Once again, I couldn't fully understand the dynamics of the moment. I don't, for instance, know what odors the dogs found in their intense, prolonged study of my hands and my clothes. I had often announced events to them by letting them smell me — for instance, after a birth I would always let them smell my hands and always noted that whatever they found there made them seem mildly curious and uncertainly joyful. I assumed they found the traces of some birth matter such as amniotic fluid and realized what it meant. So perhaps death, like birth, has characteristic odors. Or perhaps the dogs saw my face and knew that something had gone wrong. I wasn't crying, although I certainly felt sad. Dogs can observe even the slightest changes in people's demeanor, and their capacity for empathy helps them to interpret what they see. Where, after all, was Zooey? Anyway, whatever the dogs may or may not have found by way of odor, or whatever they may have thought of my appearance, they must have suspected that Zooey was far away. Not long after I left, they began howling, and they howled intermittently all night.

WHAT DO DOGS want most? They want to belong, and they want each other. Groups that form naturally, the children of a mated pair, are probably the most stable, but groups such as ours, which include a dog or two from the outside, can also be stable. Every dog might wish to be Dog One, but like us, most dogs want membership in the group even more than they want supremacy over others, so that as soon as each dog is content with his place, the social system must seem reassuringly solid to them, firm and dependable, like a good, strong ladder. Loss of a member then becomes deeply significant, which is why our dogs called to the night sky for Zooey.

Interestingly enough, the howl was one of very few pieces of obvious evidence for their powerful feelings of unity. Also in Virginia, another piece of evidence presented itself very dramatically, but the importance was inferential. The dogs made a den.

To understand why this is important, and what it might mean, we should think of our own species and how we would react if what happened to these dogs should happen to us. What would we do, for instance, if eight or nine of us were dropped off somewhere in the woods, assuming that we were to stay for a while, that we weren't obliged to find our way elsewhere, and that our situation didn't deeply distress us?

To answer the question, we'd have to know what we meant to one another. If we considered one another adversaries or suspicious-looking strangers, we would probably scatter to the four winds. If we were a team or a family, however, whether we expected to stay for a while or merely to figure out how to cope with our situation, our first act would probably be to make a camp. We would feel the need for a focus for our group and our activities. Whether we would make some kind of shelter, or clear some grass, or build a fire, or merely spread a blanket for a picnic, we would invariably alter the environment a little in a way that suited us. We would strongly, acutely feel the need to do that *first,* before we went searching for food or played a game or did whatever else seemed suitable to the occasion. Why? Because only with an established camp would we know where to place ourselves, where to come back to, where we could expect to find the others and they to find us.

To feel the need to prepare a campsite in such a situation seems so obvious to most human beings as to be almost unworthy of mention, and no wonder. The need is very old, far older than our species. Surely the idea of using a central focal area, if only as a place where the young await the foraging adult or adults, is as old as the nesting dinosaurs and perhaps much older, so that today the variety of creatures using certain spots to keep their groups together is wide indeed — from nests to camps to dens, from crocodiles to birds to dogs to people. That my dogs made a den in Virginia should not have come as a surprise.

But it did. One day we discovered what was surely the height of our dogs' achievements toward creating their own social cohesion: in spite of the numerous, comfortable, and substantial shelters we had provided for them — nice, dry shelters, some with small doors for shelter in winter, others wide open for breezy shade in summer, each shelter complete with hay and cedar shavings — the dogs had made themselves a den fully as ambitious and as brilliantly executed as any wolf den on Baffin. In fact, the den in Virginia was almost exactly like a wolf den, a tunnel penetrating horizontally for fifteen feet into the side of a hill. The dogs had chosen a well-drained place in compact, claylike earth, and had shaped the tunnel's ceiling like a shallow dome so that it wouldn't collapse on them. On one side of the tunnel near its far end they had excavated a chamber approximately three feet wide, two feet high, and three feet deep — big enough for a dog or two to sleep in.

What was most amazing about the den, though, or at least what seemed most amazing to me, was the secrecy that surrounded it. I visited the pen every day at least twice, usually much oftener, and I made a practice of walking all around it, checking for problems and possible attempts at escape. I also spent time with the dogs each day, either observing them or simply sitting in their presence, enjoying their company. Yet neither I nor any other person had the faintest notion that the dogs were working on their enormous excavation, even though the tunnel's entrance was only twenty yards from our front door. To be sure, now and then a dog or two would vanish mysteriously, but the pen was so large that they could have been elsewhere in it, and I never searched it so thoroughly that I could have said positively that the dogs in question weren't there. That the vanished dogs were deep in the earth simply never occurred to me, even though I might have been standing directly above them. Not even piles of excavated dirt betrayed their project; incredibly, they scattered more than six cubic yards of it, enough to fill a large dump truck, so carefully and so efficiently that no telltale mounds remained.

Was the secrecy intentional? I'm convinced that it was. The tunnel's entrance, for instance, was hidden underneath a woodpile, which in turn was sheltered by the eaves of our garage, which formed part of the fence of the pen. The eaves would keep rain from running into the entrance, so other considerations besides secrecy may have figured in the plan, but unless the dogs wanted secrecy it is hard to explain why they never worked on the tunnel or even went in or out of it when a person was present.

One day, though, Maria slipped up. She had already started into the entrance when I came into the pen, and when I happened to glance at the woodpile I was astonished to see her rump and tail disappearing between two of the logs. Now why would a dog squeeze down inside a woodpile? She had moved fairly smoothly, without the excitement she would have shown if she had been chasing, say, a small animal taking refuge there. Furthermore, the pile represented only the few trees we had cleared to build the garage. It was only about three logs deep, and the logs were fairly small in diameter, so that the whole pile didn't stand quite as high as a dog's shoulder. Yet Maria had vanished inside it as if by illusion. What was happening here?

I went over to look, and found a space about ten inches wide between two of the logs. I moved them, revealing a similar space between the logs below. I moved them too, and underneath I found a great, gaping, elliptic hole shaped like the underside of a bridge and its reflection, twenty-two inches across the minor axis — about the diameter of a dog. Well! I got down on my hands and knees and tried to look inside, but about three feet in, the shaft curved slightly upward, so I couldn't see very far. And it was dark. I still hadn't fully understood the implications of what I was looking at when suddenly Maria popped up face to face with me. She looked startled. I was startled too. Somewhere inside was a space big enough for her to turn around in.

We then investigated the tunnel, probed it with a

long bamboo pole, learned its size, and marveled. We also saw reasons other than social reasons for digging a den. Deep in the earth, for instance, is the perfect climate. Always a constant temperature, about fifty-five degrees Fahrenheit year round, a den seems cool in summer but warm in winter and is always a refuge from the wind, mosquitoes, and the sun. So it was easy to see why the dogs liked it. What wasn't so obvious was the secrecy. Dogs are like wolves and wolves keep their dens secret, so the secrecy wasn't unprecedented, but why have it at all? Of course, the enormous amount of energy spent on the digging gives a den genuine economic value, so perhaps the owners fear that it will be taken from them. After all, the easy way to get a den is to let others dig it and then drive them off. Or perhaps the dogs felt a wolfish atavism to protect and hide their young of the future, even though all the important females had been spayed by that time.

Whatever the reason, once the dogs knew I knew about the den, they dropped their security measures and came and went freely. Sometimes three or four dogs would go inside together and stay a long time, surely lined up one behind the other like peas in a pod. Only one, the last to enter, was sure to be staying voluntarily. The dogs deeper inside sometimes seemed to be staying simply because they couldn't get past the outer dog to freedom. No dog seemed particularly sensitive to the problem, either. Often after a long sojourn inside the tunnel, one dog would emerge calm and refreshed, but then two other, very agitated dogs might pop out right behind him and shake or run off somewhere, their fur full of dirt. They couldn't have been truly suffocating, since air could reach them through the corners of the ellipse, but after an hour or so with three dogs breathing, the tunnel probably seemed pretty close.

The den was the dogs' crowning achievement, and the focus of their lives. Eventually, trails radiated from it to all corners of the pen. As if the dogs were wolves, Maria and one of the males — her second son, Windigo — made most use of the den. They, but not the others, frequently improved it by digging it deeper. We would know that one of them was working inside it when little showers of dirt came flying out of its mouth. In keeping with the idea that subordinate animals are but satellites of the alpha pair, the other females rarely used the den at all, and little Viva, the dingo and lowest-ranking female, never used it. Instead, with the highest-ranking male, Suessi, these females stayed very near and scraped alternate beds for themselves around it, in the dirt on the hill.

And as if they had removed themselves at last

from their ties with our species, the dogs seemed to have erased human beings from their consciousness. They were always nice to us, and had never been submissive to us, but we began to feel a difference even from that. When we returned from an absence, for instance, they greeted us very mildly, if at all, and they took no notice whatever of strangers. A burglar robbed the house, but the dogs saw no problem in his presence, although a similar burglary years before in Cambridge had left Koki in a state of nervous collapse, so that while the young man burgled, she cringed in terror behind a toilet, having chosen the smallest space in the smallest, darkest room as a place to hide. But in the woods in Virginia, on the hillside by the den, her dog's life had absorbed her utterly, so that the doings of people had faded from her mind. For Koki, who had grown up as a slave, that was quite a step.

At this time, my observations almost came to an end. There was no longer anything to see. No more did the dogs interact with one another in a manner observable to human beings; like the wild wolves of Baffin, they had their relationships all ironed out. Each dog had a place, all were content, their routines were perfected, and their life was smooth and serene. Since they wouldn't react to me beyond bland, friendly acknowledgment of my presence, and since they no longer had cause to react to one another, I had no choice but to visit them in their place and on their terms. So that year in early autumn I began to spend late afternoons in the pen with them. This proved to be a remarkable experience, yet not one that can be readily described. When dogs feel serene and pleased with life, they do nothing. So there on the hillside, in the warm autumn afternoons, nothing was what we did.

Like most people who hunger to know more about the lives of animals, I have always wanted to enter into the consciousness of a nonhuman creature. I would like to know what the world looks like to a dog, for instance, or sounds like, or smells like. I would like to visit a dog's mind, to know what he's thinking and feeling, to have another dog look at me and see not something different but something the same. And to my great surprise, during those afternoons by the den, I felt I came close to achieving that.

What was it like? Partly it was like entering a quiet little village in some faraway country, and partly it was like entering another world, a new dimension. There we were, within fifty feet of my house, yet in a world that had nothing to do with my house, nothing to do with my species, and nothing to do with my life.

To sit idly, not doing, merely experiencing, comes hard to a primate, yet for once I wasn't among primates. At last, as dogs learn to live among our kind, it came to me to live among theirs. In the late afternoon sun we sat in the dust, or lay on our chests resting on our elbows, evenly spaced on the hilltop, all looking calmly down among the trees to see what moved there. No birds sang, just insects. Off in the silent, drying woods a tree would now and then drop something — a pod, perhaps, or a leaf — and we would listen to it scratching down. While the shadows grew long we lay calmly, feeling the moment, the calmness, the warm light of the red sun — each of us happy enough with the others, unworried, each of us quiet and serene. I've been to many places on the earth, to the Arctic, to the African savannah, yet wherever I went, I always traveled in my own bubble of primate energy, primate experience, and so never before or since have I felt as far removed from what seemed familiar as I felt with these dogs, by their den. Primates feel pure, flat immobility as boredom, but dogs feel it as peace.

THE STABILITY of the group was never again disrupted, but the group itself changed. Inookshook, the large, low-ranking beauty, the youngest dingo daughter, had a litter with Suessi, the high-ranking male, but pregnancy did not elevate her. Maria kept the den for herself and never thought to share it with Inookshook, who, with her foster mother, Koki, searched through the woods for a substitute. They found one under the upflung roots of a fallen tree, a shallow cavity that a colony of rats had occupied. It made me think of a hollow log I once saw in Ontario, which a pregnant young wolf without status had used in place of a den. Koki evicted the rats and Inookshook took the cavity, but at the last minute I lost courage and brought both Koki and Inookshook inside. They didn't want to be inside — they wanted their cavity — but I was afraid that the birth might go wrong, so I insisted. Five fine pups were born. Koki and Inookshook raised them together, but without the help of the main group, who stayed aloof. All the pups had been spoken for, and when they were old enough all went to their new homes.

At that time I took Inookshook and Viva to be spayed. Something went wrong with Viva. Perhaps the veterinarian overdosed her with anesthesia and destroyed her liver or her kidneys, or perhaps he removed something other than her uterus, but when I went to pick her up (I soon realized the doctor was afraid I wouldn't pay him if she died on his premises), she was barely able to stand. But she wanted to stand. She was afraid I would leave her. I will always remember the hateful veterinarian and his horrible wife trying to tell me that Viva was all right. I took her home, and after she stabilized a little so that she could travel, I took her to New

Hampshire, to the best veterinarian we knew. Even he couldn't help her. Viva knew how ill she was, and finding a dark corner in the basement of the house we were visiting, she curled up there to hide. I sat with her. Nevertheless, she suffered badly, and unable to eat or drink or to move without crying, she died at the vet's from a lethal injection to end her pain.

Two weeks later my daughter was terribly hurt in an accident and was hospitalized in Massachusetts. When my husband and I saw that our daughter wouldn't be leaving the hospital anytime soon, I moved back to Cambridge to be with her. My husband took an apartment in Washington near his job, and we rented our house to a stranger. That was the end of the dogs.

Or so it seemed. A friend with sled dogs placed Suessi and Windigo on his team, which was very good for them since they loved racing, and I found an apartment that allowed pets. It was a tiny apartment, not much bigger than the doghouse in the pen, but into it we squeezed, me, our son, a student named J. who was living with us at the time, and Koki, Inookshook, Maria, and Fatima. After a while our daughter joined us too, continuing at the hospital as an outpatient.

Maria's first act in the new apartment was to break out and go voyaging with Fatima, as she had done long ago with Misha. Where did she go? Straight back to our old neighborhood, which she hadn't seen for many years. But for an unknown reason she didn't go to our former house. Perhaps because of her flawed navigational ability she couldn't quite find it. She came close, but she gave up. With stout little Fatima faithfully at her heels, she climbed the doorstep of some exceedingly kind people who lived about two blocks away from our old place. They called me up, just as Maria had envisioned. Perhaps she had been thinking of happier times, perhaps of her den, perhaps of her sons, perhaps of Misha. Anyway, she was subdued when I went and got her.

A year went by. Our daughter got free of the hospital and went to college. The rest of us could then return to Virginia with what was left of our group. I recovered Suessi and Windigo and we went home. We weren't there long before Koki, full of years, developed stomach cancer. When she was so ill she couldn't walk, when I wanted to keep her safe and warm and as comfortable as possible with me inside the house, she longed to go back to the pen and eventually crawled there, dragging herself over the gravel to the gate, which she asked me with her eyes to open for her. I was exceedingly fond of Koki, so I stayed with her while she did what she wanted to do, which was to lie near the den. She meant so much to me that under the circumstances I probably didn't make the right observations. Nevertheless, even at that point I couldn't help but notice that in her hour of need it wasn't me she saw as helping her, although she certainly didn't seem to mind my presence. I think that once she won acceptance from the other dogs, she was afraid to lose it. She also wanted Inookshook, who sat nearby, not attending to Koki but merely there. Yet this was what Koki wanted. Near the group she had worked so hard to join, she seemed content. So for her last days of life I stayed in the pen with her. I remembered reading of dying animals who, like Viva, creep away from their group, perhaps to hide their condition from others who would compete with them. Perhaps so. Koki was different. She died without unlocking these mysteries.

Within a year, Windigo died of kidney failure, like his brother, Zooey. And then Maria developed cancer. Fatima suffered terribly from the change in Maria. She guarded her when she was sick, and when I took Maria to the vet for the last time, Fatima tried to save her and got into the car. When

I tried to evict her, she jumped into the back seat. When I opened the back door and reached for her, she jumped into the front. When I got her out at last and sped away, she ran after the car. I saw her in the rearview mirror, spinning down the road behind us like an autumn leaf.

SOON AFTER, we left Virginia and moved home to New Hampshire with what remained of us: me and my husband, with the eldest of the husky children, Suessi, and the dingo sisters, Fatima and Inookshook. Not in New Hampshire did the dogs need a pen. Instead, we installed a dog door, and we all came and went as we pleased. Like elderly inmates in a retirement community, the dogs spent quite a lot of time together, showing by their calm acceptance of one another that all conflicts had long since been resolved. Each morning they would

slowly make their way outside to urinate coopera-
tively, with Inookshook, as the lowest in their hierarchy, selecting the spot. She would nose around
until she found a place that seemed suitable, then
would urinate on it while the others waited, looking
on. Finished, she would straighten up and step aside
to wait while Fatima slowly squatted over the same
spot. When Fatima finished, Suessi would calmly
take her place and, wobbling on three legs, absently
relieve himself downward, his mind elsewhere, his
ears partly folded and his eyes half shut. Afterward
the three dogs would wander off to the top of a high,
bare hill from which they could see in all directions.
There they would spend the day lying down, view-
ing the passing scene together. Sometimes in the evening deer would come out of the woods to graze at
the edge of the field behind them, a fact in which
they took very little interest. Turning their rumps to
the deer, they mildly watched the road for other
dogs. Even in New Hampshire, where the nearest
dog neighbor was half a mile away, the group was
more interested in the social scene of their new environment than in its hunting possibilities. Thus the
long dog story seemed to be coming to a predictable
and peaceful end.

Just then, however, matters took an unexpected
turn. Out in our field, we began to notice a coyote.

Showing little concern for the elderly dogs, the coyote came to hunt voles, but before starting work would lie still for a long time in the grass looking toward the house. The dogs, with their cloudy eyes and mildly running noses, seemed unaware that anyone was watching them.

One day we mowed the field. Many small creatures, especially grasshoppers, get cut up by a mowing machine, and many wild animals seem to know it. Hardly had the mower finished its work in the late afternoon than the coyote was in the field, its head down, moving slowly along as if grazing. It had come to eat the corpses. Suddenly the dogs noticed the intruder, who was unusually conspicuous on the short grass. Without a thought for their own safety, the three dogs streamed down into the field. Afraid of a fight in which all combatants could be seriously injured, I tried to call the dogs back. But they had never been particularly inclined to obedience, especially if they felt that what they were doing was important. They kept going, while the coyote stood up very tall and straight and stiffly awaited their approach. Sure that a terrible fight was imminent, I ran too, thinking to scare the coyote. But to my great surprise, the dogs stopped short about thirty feet from the coyote, spread out over the newly mowed grass, and calmly began to eat whatever it was that the coyote had been eating. The coyote, too, returned to its food. These dogs and this coyote knew one another.

As autumn came, I sometimes saw Suessi and the coyote trotting along in single file in the shadows at the edge of the woods. Obviously, she was a female. When winter came, I found tracks that could have been their tracks together in the snow. And on a moonlit February night when the foxes were rutting, I heard a coyote's voice in the woods and wondered if she was calling Suessi. Evidently he thought so: when I went to look for him to see if he had heard the voice, I found the dog door swinging and Suessi gone.

Then what? Spring came without another sighting of the coyote. I didn't even notice her tracks. That in itself was not surprising — like most wild animals, she seemed to know about tracks. We had noticed that when snow lay on the ground, she would wait for a snowfall to change her range from the west side of the road to the east side, so that any tracks she might leave on the road would be visible for only a few moments before being hidden by snow. Meanwhile, however, other coyotes came and went in our fields, often in the company of their scouts, the northern ravens. It almost seemed that in the coyote world, our woods and fields were changing ownership quite often. But where had Suessi's coyote gone? Surely she had gotten pregnant, since by spring most adult female coyotes are pregnant, usually by their consorts. In her case, the consort seemed to have been Suessi. This meant, however, that she would have the difficult task of raising her children on her own, without the help of their father — something that female coyotes who mate with dogs are inevitably faced with, which contributes to infant mortality, which in turn explains why the coyote population stays relatively pure, with fewer coydogs than might otherwise be expected.

So perhaps she was being extra careful about showing herself, since she was the sole support of her children. Coyotes know, of course, that they are hated by many people. One day a former game warden of our area actually boasted that he had dug out and killed a coyote and her children from a den in a national wildlife sanctuary that abuts our land. He didn't even realize he had broken the law, since to him, coyotes weren't deserving of protection. We didn't know which coyote he had killed, of course, but we saw Suessi's pretty lady no more. Even so, as time passed, we began to think that the tragically and illegally murdered coyote was a stranger and that Suessi's coyote had not only survived but managed to raise at least one child. A year later, among the voyagers in the shadows at the edge of the field was a splendid young coyote whose fur was very pale, like Suessi's, and who had one lopped ear, like Suessi's father, Misha. We then convinced ourselves that he was Suessi's son. Best of all, one day three ravens flew down into the field and strode around all afternoon hunting something, perhaps voles. That evening the pale coyote came into the field with these ravens, which made us think he might be purposefully associating himself with them, as if, perhaps, he had scouts of his own.

Or so we told ourselves. As dogs get old, one likes to think of continuity. Who will be like them in the future? Who was like them in the past? As Inookshook got gray with age, for instance, long dark stripes appeared on her sides like shadows in her fading fur. Apparently these stripes had been there all along, but so faint that her gorgeous color had masked them. No other dogs in this hemisphere have such stripes, as far as I know; they were regular, broad, and on the diagonal, like the stripes below a zebra's waist, except that Inookshook's stripes slanted down and back, withers to groin, whereas a zebra's stripes slant up and back, from breastbone to hips. In fact, the only time I'd ever seen such stripes on a dog was on a wild dingo in Australia. A formidable great creature, this dingo had been on a hillside lying down behind a rock, contemplating some calves in a drying billabong below. His dark stripes camouflaged him beautifully, but not so well that the cows couldn't see him. Mindful of their children, they were standing on tiptoes and craning their necks to peer at him suspiciously over the top of the rock. I liked to think that Inookshook's stripes came from Australia by way of her dingo mother. Anyway, this seemed more likely than an inheritance from her husky father, even though most dingoes don't have stripes but are, of course, red-gold, the color of Australian grass. Yet Asian pye-dogs sometimes have stripes, and now and then even today an Asian pye-dog finds its way to Australia, usually as a passenger on some leaking coastal vessel, or even in an oceangoing canoe. So the Asian ancestor, too, was good to think of, however humble — a reminder that since ancient times, the dog family has redefined itself again and again, often through meetings at the edges of fields, all over the world.

What do dogs want? They want each other. Human beings are merely a cynomorphic substitute, as we all know. Dogs who live in each other's company are calm and pragmatic, never showing the desperate need to make known their needs and feelings or to communicate their observations, as some hysterical dogs who know only the company of our species are likely to do. Dogs who live in each other's company know they are understood. Inookshook at the end of her life had forgotten almost everything she had ever learned about our species, from our identities to her own housebreaking skills, yet she went on about life calmly with Suessi and Fatima, accepting her responsibilities to them as her duty and her place with them as her right. Fatima too felt her strongest obligations to her stepbrother, Suessi, and her half-sister, Inookshook. After an overnight stay at the School of Veterinary Medicine at Cornell, where I had taken her to see what could be done about her diabetes, she marched straight from her hospital cage through the door of the clinic and out to the car that would take her back to her family, and she wasted not even a look at me or anyone else. This came as a great surprise to the veterinarians, who had been expecting a tearful reunion. And

Suessi, who by the end of his life was almost crazy with Alzheimer's disease, had nearly forgotten that human beings existed. He knew the coyotes in the woods and the voles in the fields and he knew about his sisters, the dingo ladies, but he would sometimes look at us with a puzzled expression, as if he had forgotten not only who we were but also what we were.

Suessi died one winter from a lethal injection to end his suffering from arthritis, which at the time of his death had become so severe that he couldn't stand up. I took him to the veterinarian in our town, and his death was almost as peaceful as the death of a tree. He faded quickly and was gone. At home I showed the other dogs his collar. I happened to be standing with them in my office, a bare, unheated room attached to our garage, where, after examining the collar, Fatima and Inookshook slowly moved their nostrils over me, carefully investigating all the odors that clung to my hands and my clothes. When they had finished, they both stepped back and looked at me quietly, as if thinking things over, or taking things in. Then, as we stood there together in the cold, bright room, just gazing at one another, they suddenly began to emit an odor. It was the odor of dog, of wet dog, musky and penetrating, and it was rising like a cloud of cold steam from one or both of the two dingo sisters, seeping through their skins, growing stronger and stronger until the room was filled with it. I had never experienced anything similar before, and had no idea what was happening. I have no idea now. But as we stood there quietly looking at one another in the icy room, in the overwhelming cloud of odor, it came to me that death and odor go together, not as corruption but as memory — or at least they do with dogs. As voices travel where their makers can't go, so odors cling where their makers can't stay. The odor was a dog thing. I couldn't pretend to understand it. But interestingly enough, my body responded to it: the hair rose on my skin.

Inookshook died a few weeks later, also unconscious and peaceful, also like a dying tree. Then Fatima lived on alone. I've known dogs who searched or called or waited for their dead owners, but Fatima did none of these things. She knew what had happened to Suessi and Inookshook. As her diabetes worsened, she of course grew less active, but otherwise she seemed reasonably accepting of the way things were. She even learned that insulin made her feel better, although the injection took an hour or more to take effect. Somehow she managed to associate the injection with the comfort that resulted much later, so that when the time came for her shot, she would nudge us for it as a dog sometimes nudges for food. A despondent dog could never figure out something as obscure as that. (Nor was she the only dog ever to do this. At least one other dog in our community has done the same.)

Even so, I believe Fatima felt that her life was over. One day she simply walked off into the woods and disappeared. Of course we missed her right away and then searched intensively, not only by ourselves but also with many other people and with three other dogs. We called the local and state police, the humane society, and all the veterinarians, we posted notices everywhere that people gather, and we advertised in all the newspapers and on the radio, offering a reward. But our efforts were absolutely useless. Surely Fatima had felt her death coming and had gone off to meet it, and although year after year our search continues, we have never found the slightest trace of her, not even her collar or her bones.

ALTHOUGH I am deeply indebted to others for the material in this book, to begin by thanking my conspecifics would be reminiscent of, say, early works of anthropology wherein the author gratefully acknowledges the help of his colleagues and the colonial officials but forgets to thank the people who were most helpful to the study, the patient villagers who taught him how to talk and act, who let him see their ceremonies and who answered his questions. But I don't want to emulate the hypothetical anthropologist. Unlike him, I know who helped me the most, in my case ten dogs and a dingo, and so I begin by thanking them, particularly Misha, Maria, and Koki, also Suessi, Fatima, and Viva.

Now perhaps I seem like the early anthropologist after all. In real life in anthropology, the most helpful people often come from the social extremes, the high-ranking people because they are the bosses, and without their cooperation nothing gets done, and the low-ranking people because whatever stigmatizes them in their own society doesn't register with the alien investigator, who, as an outsider, befriends them without prejudice. In exchange for recognition and friendship, the low-ranking people reward the investigator with information. Interestingly, most people seem to act like this just about everywhere, all over the world. Even more interestingly, dogs do too. High-ranking dogs may monopolize a human being, keeping their social inferiors away. The human, after all, is a valuable commodity — almost a trophy. Meanwhile, the human being is poorly adapted for discerning rank in dogs, and is just as likely to befriend a low-ranking dog as any other. Low status does not mean low intelligence; the stigmatized dog usually understands the situation at once and avails himself of the human being's high status.

In my village, the chiefs were Misha and Maria, Koki, Suessi, and, years later, Fatima. So in recognizing their contribution and in thanking them for it, I am doing what the early anthropologist would have done after all: kowtowing to power.

And Viva? A dingo, Viva was like a dog, but more so. What the dogs did inconspicuously, Viva did dramatically. As a result, like the early anthropologist's best informant, she showed me many unexpected things I otherwise might have missed — for instance, the fact that dogs feel differently about their front feet and their hind feet. Once when water from a hose flowed around her, she picked up her front feet one by one to shake them while ignoring her hind feet, which stood in water to the ankles. Viva also used her front feet like hands to manipulate things.

Being from a different tribe than the other dogs, Viva was isolated from them. Her isolation gave her low status, so she was lonely. In the society of dogs, I too was an outsider, and she saw this, and often clung to me for companionship. Once when we were moving to a new home, I put her in a pen lest she run away or get under the wheels of the van, yet the swarm of strange people plus the upheaval and confusion upset her so much that she tried to bite and claw her way to freedom. She was showing me that dogs when very distressed must do something, anything, as long as they take some kind of action. I was afraid that she'd get out, and went to fix the hole she had made. When she realized what I meant to do, she frantically tried to force her way out through the hole before I could prevent her. When I pushed her head and shoulders back inside and started to mend the hole with wire, she grabbed my sleeve and, her eyes riveted on mine, grabbed again, filling her mouth to the molars with the cloth, and when she had a really good grip, she threw herself backward and pulled with all her strength, trying to pull me in with her. She was so strong she pulled me flat against the wire, but I was too big to fit through the hole. She stopped pulling then, but didn't release her grip. She just held me tight against the cage and looked at me for a while. In time, she was able to accept that her plan had been a failure. Then gradually and reluctantly she opened her mouth and let me go.

Not everything she did was understandable, at least not to human beings. When she traveled with me in a car, for instance, she knew when we were about to reach our destination even if she had not been there before, and waking from her long, bored sleep, she would brighten visibly and look out the window. The bumpiness of the road after the car went off the interstate and onto country byways was a clue, but not the only clue; often the destination was reached over many miles of unimproved surface. The repeated turns a car makes onto increasingly smaller roads and driveways near the end of a trip were also a clue, but often Viva brightened for arrival before the car began turning. When I realized she was accurately predicting most of our arrivals, I tried to make sure that I myself wasn't giving a cue, either by speaking or by doing something different, and I believe I succeeded in hiding my feelings. She still knew, though, and by the end of her life I was no closer to figuring out how she did it than I had been at the beginning. Dog ESP? Perhaps. Yet at one time, the ability of elephants to communicate over great distances was half-jokingly attributed to ESP. In fact, elephants communicate with long-distance calling, loud but too low for people to hear. However, although people had kept elephants as slaves for more than 2,500 years, no one knew about the infrasound until 1983. So perhaps dogs, who are unsurpassed observers, may perceive things about us or about the world that would surprise us. Perhaps for all my care I was, after all, doing something, either with myself or with the car, that gave little Viva the clue. And so, although I'll always be grateful to her for many things, I'm especially grateful that she brought out this mystery, perhaps the most typical gift that animals give us when we study their behavior. Without animals like Viva, we can't even identify what we don't know.

I am also indebted to numerous people, most of all my husband, my children, Peter Lynch, Pat Sterret Stokes, and Peter Thomas, dog owners extraordinaire, whose cooperation and forbearance made the effort possible. I am deeply indebted to Dave Houston and his family for showing us how to put together a sled dog team. I learned more about sled dogs from Dave than from any other person, and the sport gave enormous pleasure to us all, people and dogs alike. I would also like to express my gratitude for the lifelong skill and care of the late Dr. Forrest F. Tenney, who as a young veterinarian cared for my first dog in 1940. I would like to thank Dr. Michael Maki and Dr. Charles DeVinne for their great skill, friendship, and compassion. Incredibly, dogs actually enjoy visiting these veterinarians and go in for their appointments with their heads and tails high. I also want to thank Mert Dyer, our selectman and representative to the state legislature and until recently the pharmacist of our town, for his extreme kindness in obtaining an unusual form of insulin that we needed in tiny quantities for Fatima. The profit to the pharmacy must have been zero, and the trouble of getting the insulin must have been great. It would have been easy to say the insulin was unobtainable and thereby to save a lot of trouble, especially since the patient was just an animal. But instead, month after month, Mert found us the insulin we needed and Fatima lived on. For generously trying to help me find Fatima after she had vanished, I would like to thank Gretchen Poisson.

The debt of this book to the illustrator, Jared Williams, is very obvious, yet I would like to thank him as much for his interest as for his art. For generously allowing the use of the photographs that inspired certain of the drawings, I would like to thank the photographer Peter Schweitzer. For her unfailing perfection as a copy editor, now as always, I would like to thank Liz Duvall. For reading the manuscript and for their excellent advice, I would like to thank the writers Howard Mansfield and Sy Montgomery. I would also like to thank Sy for the way she writes about animals, presenting them as the individuals they are rather than as automatons that represent a species. In the same context, as well as for insight into the observational powers of animals, I would like to thank Vicki Hearne, whose many books on dogs have done much to further our understanding. I would like to thank my agent, Ike Williams, and the publisher, Peter Davison, not only for their ability and attention to this book but also because both gentlemen are so very pleasant to work with. And finally, I would like to thank Bob Gottlieb, perhaps the world's most gifted editor, whose generous enthusiasm has been very encouraging to me and to many other people, and who envisioned this material as a book.

BIBLIOGRAPHY

The following list comprises a few classic works to which I am particularly indebted.

Ackerley, J. R. 1965. My dog Tulip. New York: Poseidon Press.
Beck, Alan. 1973. The ecology of stray dogs: A study of free-ranging urban animals. Baltimore: York Press.
Clutton-Brock, Juliet. 1987. A natural history of domesticated mammals. London: British Museum.
Crisler, Lois. 1958. Arctic wild. Boston: Little, Brown.
Hearne, Vicki. 1986. Adam's task: Calling animals by name. New York: Knopf.
Mech, L. David. 1966. The wolves of Isle Royale. *Fauna of the National Parks of the United States,* Fauna Series, No. 7. Washington: Government Printing Office.
———. 1970. The wolf: The ecology and behavior of an endangered species. New York: Natural History Press.

Murie, Adolph. 1944. The wolves of Mount McKinley. *Fauna of the National Parks of the United States,* Fauna Series, No. 5. Washington: Government Printing Office.

Scott, J. P., and J. L. Fuller. 1965. Genetics and the social behavior of the dog. Chicago: University of Chicago Press.

Zeuner, Frederick E. 1963. A history of domesticated animals. New York: Harper & Row.